Bébé Gourmet

MY BABY RECIPE BOOK

100 easy recipes for raising adventurous eaters

Jenny Carenco

of Les Menus Bébé

Vermilion

10 9 8 7 6 5 4 3 2 1
Published in 2013 by Vermilion, an imprint of Ebury Publishing.
First published by Marabout Editions as *Mon Livre des Recettes pour Bébé* in 2009. First published in the USA by
The Experiment in 2013. Ebury Publishing is a Random House Group company.

The Random House Group Limited Reg. No. 954009
Addresses for companies within the Random House Group can be found at
www.randomhouse.co.uk

A CIP catalogue record for this book is available from the British Library.

The Random House Group Limited supports The Forest Stewardship Council® (FSC®), the leading international
forest-certification organisation. Our books carrying the FSC label are printed on FSC®-certified paper. FSC is the only
forest-certification scheme supported by the leading environmental organisations, including Greenpeace. Our paper
procurement policy can be found at www.randomhouse.co.uk/environment

ISBN 978 0091 954727

Copies are available at special rates for bulk orders. Contact the sales development team on 020 7840 8487 for more
information. To buy books by your favourite authors and register for offers, visit www.randomhouse.co.uk

This book contains the opinions and ideas of its author. It is intended to provide helpful and informative material on the
subjects addressed in the book. The information in this book has been compiled by way of general guidance in relation to the
specific subjects addressed, but is not a substitute and not to be relied on for medical, healthcare, pharmaceutical or other
professional advice on specific circumstances and in specific locations. So far as the author is aware the information given is
correct and up to date as at September 2013. Practice, laws and regulations all change, and the reader should obtain up-to-
date professional advice on any such issues. The author and publishers disclaim, as far as the law allows, any liability arising
directly or indirectly from the use, or misuse, of the information contained in this book.

Cover design by Two Associates
Cover photographs by Frédéric Lucano
Author photograph by Jean-Claude Amiel
Food styling by Sonia Lucano
Recipe testing by Alisa Morov
Text design by Marabout

Colour origination by Altaimage, London. Printed and bound in China by Toppan Leefung.

For Maya and Milo . . .

Contents

first compotes & first purées

first lunches & first sweets

first dinners

AUTHOR'S NOTE

*T*his is not the story of one of those perfect mothers who, for some reason the rest of us will never understand, manages to put a home-made meal on the table every night, including home-baked rolls that she prepares without ever breaking one of her perfectly manicured nails. This is *my* story, the story of your average Super Mum. She wants the best for her children and through trial and error has found a way to cook tasty and nutritious meals for her baby – without leaving her job, reducing her nightly sleep to two hours or hiring round-the-clock staff. This book is the fruit of my kitchen adventures; it is my personal notebook, the essence of my baby-feeding years, the results of my trials, the shortcuts and tricks that I found to make cooking for my kids a fun and relatively easy way to share my passion for good food and healthy eating.

My story starts six months after my daughter Maya was born. Introducing my little angel to her first foods had suddenly crawled its way to the top of my priority list, so I happily made my way down the baby-food aisle of my favourite supermarket to choose what was going to be Maya's first experience with solid food. 'Peas' read one label. *Wonderful*, I thought, *I love peas and I know how nutritious and fibre-rich they are*. Yet, how strangely grey the purée looked. What was *really* in there? I took a closer look at the label. Water, starch and just 22 per cent peas? And the labels went on like this – row after row, shelf after shelf, disappointment after disappointment. *This* is what we're feeding our kids in France, the country whose gastronomy made the United Nations World Heritage List? I was stunned. Needless to say, I left the supermarket empty-handed, and a little bit troubled as I knew that (a) I was never going to feed Maya those peas from the baby-food aisle, (b) I was supposed to start working in five days, and (c) I had little-to-no knowledge about how to cook baby food myself.

The other half of my brain told me everything was going to be fine! I love cooking. Baby food might require a slightly different set of skills from pulling together dinner for my husband and myself, not to mention consideration of food sensitivities and avoiding potential allergies, but I had the strongest tool of all: motivation. *Pea purée?* I can make that! *Beef stew for babies?* Hmm … I guess I can cook some up. *Baby-friendly fish casserole?* Okay, I would have to research that one, but it couldn't be impossible. I was determined to figure it all out when I got home, and even made a promise to Maya:

'Mum is going to cook yummy little dishes for you, and you're going to learn to love all the wonderful fruits, veggies and other foods that your dad and I do. You're going to bite into life with curiosity and appetite; you're going to be healthy and happy. I want you to be an adventurous eater, my child!'

Later that night, when my family was sleeping, I started to study the art of cooking for my baby. It wasn't as complicated as I thought. Fears of food allergies, intolerances, choking, rashes and the other scenarios I had drawn up in my head quickly vanished and I began to think up recipe ideas for Maya. We started with the basics: carrots, green beans, peas, pumpkin, broccoli … and Maya loved them all! My husband and I like our meals well seasoned, so I started to add a little spice or some herbs to Maya's food – a pinch of cumin in with the carrots, a few basil leaves in the green beans. She was thrilled with these new additions. And *I* was thrilled that I needed to spend only an hour or two on Sunday preparing Maya's meals for the entire week. I simply popped them into the freezer until it was time to eat – and when Maya was hungry, her meals took only minutes to prepare.

Of course, not every recipe was an immediate success. I might have gone a bit overboard with that fennel and raisin risotto, or when I tried to do something interesting with smoked trout. (I will never forget Maya's reaction – or the look on the doctor's face when I told him, 'Maya loves everything but smoked trout!') But these first months of experimentation were a wonderful journey for both Maya and me, travelling through tastes and discoveries together.

Up until this point, my story resembles those of many other parents who cook. But mine was about to take another turn. It all started one day when I was visiting a friend with Maya. My friend told me that her son Hugo, eight months at the time, was really picky about food – especially green vegetables, which he pretty much refused to eat. She was curious to understand how Maya ate everything with such gusto. When I told her about my personal recipes, she asked if I would give her one of my dishes out of the freezer to test on her son. I dropped off some of my Green Bean and Sweet Pea Purée with Basil and she called back the same night, telling me that Hugo had eaten absolutely everything – and with a smile! This happened several times with different friends over the subsequent months. People wanted to know my secret. At one point I thought to myself, *Why is there no alternative between bottled baby food (quick and practical but not necessarily tasty) and home-made baby food (tasty but sometimes time-consuming to make)?* I went home that evening and told my husband that I wanted to leave my stable and well-paid job as a strategy consultant and start a baby-food business. He told me I was crazy and gave me the thumbs up (which is one of the reasons I love him so much).

Eighteen months, thousands of work hours, hundreds of doubts and just as many assurances later, Les Menus Bébé were available for sale at grocery shops across the Paris region. The rest is history.

What you hold in your hands is the result of several years' work. Here are my most successful attempts to bring delectable, nutritious and balanced food to my babies' table – and now to yours. You'll find all the recipes that Maya and Milo (my son, who arrived three years after Maya) loved the most, all the recipes so easy to make that even *I* couldn't find an excuse not to whip them up – all the recipes that were selected for the Les Menus Bébé line. In this book you'll also find my 'Yummy Tips' and organisational tricks for squeezing baby-food cooking into your already busy schedule, ideas for how to help your baby love all kinds of tastes and textures, and ways you can help him or her become an adventurous, happy and healthy eater.

So thank you for picking up this book. Thank you for deciding that what your baby eats is important. Thank you for believing that taste is one of the most important senses we have. Thank you for wanting to share your culinary traditions and nutritional convictions with your little one. Thank you for taking the time to help your baby learn to love all the yummy tastes of nature. Thank you, Super Parent! You're doing a great job.

Love,

Jenny

Dr Jean Lalau Keraly, paediatric nutritionist and endorinologist

Passing on the pleasure of eating

As a doctor specialising in childhood nutrition and obesity, after twenty years of experience I've noticed that the concept of pleasure is at least as important in nutrition – and in the treatment of nutrition-related illnesses – as the foods themselves. It's never too early, or too late, to introduce a child to the world of flavours. It's the one thing that will enable him or her, as an adult, to see healthy eating not as an obligation, but as a true pleasure.

Make mealtimes something special

How many times in my surgery have I listened to mothers' sighs of regret as they blame themselves for not having taken the time to prepare their baby's first purées! Commercial baby food is successful, even if none of us is foolish enough to believe that it's a cure-all. While it is practical, economical and hygienic, mass-produced baby food has a long way to go in terms of taste and creativity. Taking the time to prepare your baby's meals helps make mealtimes something special.

Ambiance and appetite

It's something I notice every day in my line of work: the environment in which a child eats determines her appetite, conditions her interest in her meal, her desire to taste and even the general way in which she understands food. A child's mealtime is all too often punctuated with bouts of crying, threats, worry and indifference. It's no wonder many babies are not so inclined to discover new foods.

Baby meals for a baby revolution

When I met Jenny Carenco during a doctor's visit, I was immediately impressed by the epicurean vision that she wanted to pass on to her daughter as well as the daring baby-food recipes she was trying out. I tried to share my knowledge of nutrition and children's health with her, and to be a source of reassurance and encouragement when she was having doubts. And like any mother who has decided to achieve something on her baby's behalf, she did amazing things! But she wanted more: to give all parents access to the baby recipes she had devised. Her objective: to reconcile – perhaps for the first time – practicality with an explosion of flavours in order to lead a new generation on the path to natural, varied and balanced foods.

(Re)discovering the pleasure of 'home-made'

The challenge was clear and I immediately jumped on board, seizing the chance to collaborate with Jenny and contribute to changing things for the better. I regularly see children in my surgery who have never bitten into an apple – children for whom the food universe consists mainly of sugary foods and pasta. Today, commercial food for children that contains added sugar – baby food included – locks our children into a reassuring, yet dangerous, spiral in which everything is sugary and uniform in taste. Supporting Jenny's gutsy project was taking a step towards the first true alternative since Gerber's 'home-made' baby-food jars appeared in 1930. It also meant offering hurried parents a real path to feeding their little ones naturally. Finally, it presented an opportunity for the beginning of a change in the general mindset and an awakening of the parental consciousness.

Taking control of your family's diet

This book completes the picture. Jenny was looking for a way to prepare balanced meals for her baby, and this book includes all that she has learnt along the way so that parents like you finally have a true resource. This book shows parents how to take control of their family's diet, from the baby to the eldest child, without giving up too much in return. It playfully expounds on the joys of eating, instilling the basics of healthy food consumption, cleverly fitting into modern parents' lifestyles and encouraging them to take an educational trip along the unknown – and somewhat frightening – path of the 'home-made'. You hold in your hands a guide to helping your children become healthy eaters – the only reliable weapon against obesity and rampant food disorders. Let's get cooking!

The secret to successful baby cuisine? organisation!

A bit clichéd, maybe, yet it's completely true. In order to keep your sanity (and get some sleep), your only life preserver is a well-thought-out plan. You'll see, by integrating the techniques and recipes into your routine bit by bit, you will be able to follow it without even thinking. And it's at this moment that you'll say to yourself, 'In fact, making food for my brood is not witchcraft!' But before we get there, let's do a quick theoretical trial run. A champion's logistical foundations can be enumerated on only one hand.

Rule 1: always have a supply of 'saviour foods' to hand

Why saviours? Because if you always have them in stock, they'll be your lifesavers, enabling you to pull together healthy, quick and delicious recipes for the whole family! Without these culinary basics, each recipe will feel like Mount Everest, forcing you to shop every day for one or two missing ingredients – a real nightmare for a working parent. So make sure you have a few saviour foods in your storecupboard (see pages 16–19).

Rule 2: pool recipes

Sure, you are going to cook these recipes for your baby. But look at it from another angle: the vegetables or ingredients that you're going to prepare for your budding gourmet can also serve as the basis for your own meals. That way you won't feel as though you're spending the whole night in the kitchen, dreaming up separate meals for your baby, the older children and for the evening *tête-à-tête* with your partner. Share the wealth! For almost every recipe in this book I've given you 'Yummy Tips' for transforming the baby recipe into a tasty dish for grown-ups. You can also use the chart on pages 184–5 for recipe inspiration organised by ingredients and the diner's age.

Rule 3: make extra and do less work later

Let's be honest. There are evenings when even the most organised of parents simply doesn't have the twenty minutes it takes to prepare a simple meal: think never-ending managers' meetings, massive traffic problems, incubating flu … Don't panic. The perfect planner in you has already prepared for this possibility. Just take one of your 'emergency containers' (that you made up on one of your more courageous days) out of the freezer. If you're worried you'll never have one of those courageous days to devote expressly to cooking the emergency supplies, no problem. My extreme laziness also inspired this ironclad logic; all I had to do was cook larger quantities of baby meals than I needed and freeze the leftovers. See the 'prep/cook/storage' box opposite.

Rule 4: make a weekly meal plan

Life will be so much easier if you organise your menus for the week ahead. First, you'll be able to do your shopping all at once and avoid the horror of the crowded supermarket on your way home from work. You'll also be able to plan your recipes around your schedule. Are your Tuesday nights cut short by that endless meeting your supervisor insists on holding at 6pm? Then put the osso buco on hold and use your always calm Monday evening to make Tuesday's ratatouille. In one word, *plan* in order to manage your time effectively.

Rule 5: make Sunday evenings your logistical ally

You'll tell anyone who will listen: I'm sick of Sunday night films from the eighties! Well, instead of vegetating before the umpteenth showing of *Back to the Future II*, use this night to get a head start on your weekly dinner menus. Putting on your favourite music and spending one hour in the kitchen will save you much needed time during the rest of the week – when you're likely to be feeling tired, stressed and irritable. Prepare all the sauces that need some time to simmer, then freeze them, leaving only accompaniments like pasta and couscous to cook at the last minute. To be honest, this Sunday cooking time alone with my thoughts and my music is a real escape for me. And when I have to spend only three minutes to reheat those pre-prepared meals, I'm simply ecstatic.

---

prep/cook/storage

Directly under the title of each recipe, you will notice these four symbols:

🕐   notes a recipe's prep time in minutes

🍲   notes a recipe's cooking time in minutes

🗄   notes how long a recipe can be stored in the refrigerator

❄   notes at what temperature (°C) a recipe should be frozen

🕐	🍲	🗄	❄
5	10	24^h	-18°

For example, these symbols indicate that a recipe takes 5 minutes to prep and 10 to cook, can be stored for 24 hours in the refrigerator and must be frozen at -18°C. You'll notice that all but a handful of special baking recipes at the back of the book take under 30 minutes to prep and cook, and many take under 15 minutes! If you see the ❄ symbol, you'll know that you can plan ahead according to rule 5 and freeze those meal components in advance.

ESSENTIAL TOOLS

a stick blender

You'll love this little 'giraffe', which will turn your tasty small meals into easy soups for your baby, then into thick purées and finally into chunkier compotes with morsels of whole food. Easy to use and to clean.

a large heavy-based saucepan (with lid)

Invest in this 4-in-1 utensil, which will allow you to reduce a risotto, boil water for pasta, simmer a stew and brown meat! It's perfect for small kitchens.

a vegetable peeler

Better than a knife because it peels away the flesh in a flash and keeps more of the outer skin, which contains most of the vitamins.

a potato masher or ricer

The *only* way to make a potato purée, unless you want to serve potato glue. Find one in your favourite kitchen shop.

a fine sieve and colander

For removing lumps from purées, sauces and compotes, and for draining pasta and vegetables. plastic containers in various sizes Easy to use, freeze, store and wash, these will simplify your organisation, and therefore your life.

foil

For wrapping up, poaching, baking or cooking *en papillote* (wrapped and baked in foil or baking parchment). It's an essential item in a cook's drawer.

baking parchment

It's the stuff we're always afraid to put in the oven, but it's made especially for this task – as well as for cooking without burning, for easy removal from the pan to protect food, and for cooking *en papillote*.

freezer bags with zip fasteners

Indispensable for keeping leftovers in the fridge, storing portions of baby meals or carrying snacks without having to worry about leaks.

a chopping board and a good knife

Choose a big plastic chopping board that's flexible enough to let you transfer chopped vegetables into the pan without losing half of them.

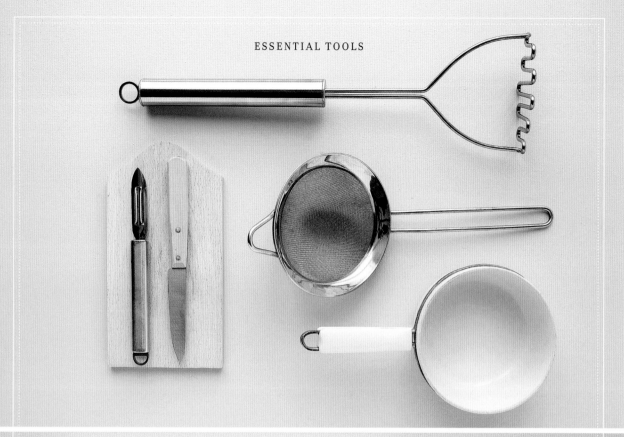

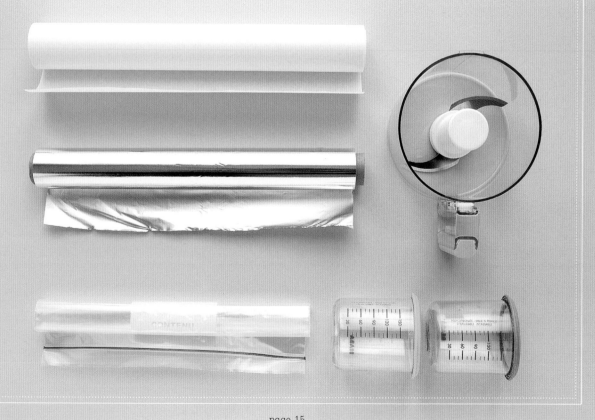

storecupboard essentials

These are your 'storecupboard essentials', the items that you use regularly and should always have to hand. Keep stock of them to make sure you never run out. A bi-monthly purchase should do it.

raisins and
sultanas

ready-to-eat
dried apricots
or prunes

clear honey

ground
cumin, ginger,
mixed spice,
cinnamon

caster sugar

baking powder

olive oil

soft brown sugar

pasta

plain flour

crunchy or plain muesli

couscous and polenta

basmati and Arborio (round Italian) rice

frozen in advance

These are your 'frozen friends', the fresh items you've frozen ahead of time to simplify your life. They will keep for a long time, yet still retain the flavour and nutritional value present in freshly picked fruits and vegetables.

summer berries and exotic fruits: mangoes, lychees, pineapple …

aromatic fresh herbs (basil, chives, tarragon, thyme and coriander) and chopped shallots and garlic

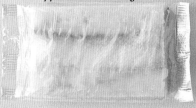

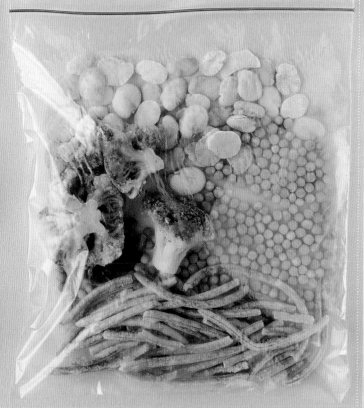

fish fillets (cod, salmon, tuna) and white chicken meat

green vegetables: peas, broccoli, broad beans, green beans, spinach

fresh dairy

This is your 'must-have' basket: the list of things you should get in the habit of buying every time you go to the supermarket. They'll become instinctive purchases.

grated Parmesan

milk

fromage frais or natural, unsweetened Greek yogurt

crème fraîche (or cream cheese will do in a pinch)

soft cheese, such as Laughing Cow

butter

fresh fruits and vegetables

Here's your ticket to healthy pleasure. Keep these treasures to hand in small quantities for meals that are rich in taste. Replenish your supply weekly.

oranges and clementines

apples

bananas

tomatoes: regular and cherry

don't forget seasonal berries!

courgettes

potatoes

carrots

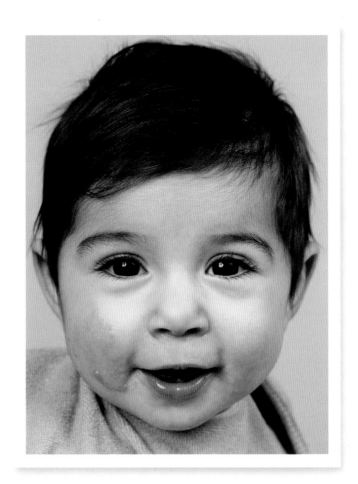

Mona,
6 months, baby foodie

first compotes
&
first purées

*starting from about 6 months of age and not
before 4 months (17 weeks)*

Dr Jean Lalau Keraly, paediatric nutritionist and endocrinologist

When should I introduce solid food?

It's the question that gnaws at parents – some worrying that their little one will be undernourished if they don't give him his first purée the day he turns four months old. Others see potential allergens everywhere – even in foods as innocuous as the green bean, so they subject it to appalling culinary transformations intended to rid the bean of its potential toxicity and its vitamins at the same time. In the UK, the current NHS guidelines recommend that parents wean their babies at around six months and not before four months (17 weeks) – but every baby is different so here are some pointers.

Listen to your baby!

You know it's time to give your baby his first fruits or vegetables when he starts to be interested in them! Does he stretch out his hand to grab at whatever's on your plate or ask for the crust of bread you're about to crunch on? Can he sit up on his own and hold his head steady? And if he has puree in his mouth, does he swallow it? If yes, it's without a doubt the time to let him taste his first compotes. Are you stamping your feet with impatience at the idea of having your six month old taste that carrot purée, even though he's still greedily sucking his bottle and clamps his mouth shut whenever you approach him with a spoonful of food? Try again later! Around the age of six months, there's no hurry; breast milk or formula remains his staple food, which will help him grow properly. The first meals are an initiation to flavours and to the pleasure of eating, not yet (or at least not very much) a real nutritional contribution.

The path to a varied diet

Fruits or vegetables first? In order to give parents a better response than 'it makes no difference', experts have divided themselves into two camps, 'veggies first' and 'fruit first', and each side has excellent arguments. As long as you introduce your little one to a food, it doesn't matter if it's a vegetable or a fruit. Simply avoid at-risk foods e.g. those with strong potential for allergies – eggs, wheat, strawberries and nuts – while your baby is under six months of age.

Let your baby follow his own rhythm

Certain parents worry when they see their baby refusing to eat the suggested foods prescribed by official nutritional guidelines. What's the difference, if their little one is in good health? During the discovery phase, offer your baby what awakens his curiosity and makes him happy. Let him get to know foods, and don't worry if he doesn't always finish the portion size prescribed by your healthcare professional; breast milk or formula will fill in any nutritional gaps.

Is he asking for more carrots?

Give him some more. Your role is to introduce him to fruits and vegetables, which is pure pleasure! Offer him fruits or veggies depending on what you're in the mood to cook as well as whatever your baby is asking for. Is it hot outside? Opt for a peach compote. It's cold? Whip up a yummy broccoli purée. Start with gentle variations, at first proposing a single new food every three or four days, in order to monitor your baby's reactions and check for allergies. If all goes well, keep going by introducing other foods.

Never force your child

If you do, you run the risk of compromising his future relationship to food. Instead, simply put out prepared fruits and vegetables, and observe his reaction to them. Finally, don't hesitate to invite your baby to join you at the dinner table so he can familiarise himself with your (positive) eating habits and enter into the 'grown-up' dynamic. And if, on top of it all, he discovers that you're eating the same thing he is, it's a pretty good bet that Baby will quickly, successfully and excitedly enter the magical world of food.

A special note to changephobes

To parents worried about the potential danger of certain foods, I'll say this: you cannot put your child in a protective bubble. The passage to solid food is a turning point in his development of motor skills. Food in itself is not dangerous, even if Baby winds up having a food allergy. Simply take your time so that Baby can get used to a range of fruits and vegetables. This way, you can control his reactions and adjust his diet according to his needs. Holding back the introduction of solid food (beyond about six months) means taking the risk of exposing your child to nutritional deficiencies or eating behaviour problems.

And a special note to the change determined

To those who want to introduce solid food early (before about six months), be aware that this means replacing a whole food – breast milk or formula – with something less nutritionally complete. It's only after this time that a baby's digestive system is mature enough to process anything other than milk. By then his intestinal mucus membrane is reinforced, reducing the risks of food allergy. The suction reflex has diminished and his muscular coordination has improved, allowing Baby to use his tongue to push the purées into his throat before swallowing them. For more advice on the current NHS guidelines visit www.nhs.uk.

NOTE: Some recipes in this chapter contain dairy products, herbs, spices and vanilla. Dairy products and herbs are not recommended for babies below the age of six months and spices and vanilla are not recommended for babies below the age of eight months.

peach compote
compote de pêches

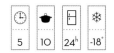

| 5 | 10 | 24ʰ | -18° |

Makes five 100g (3¹/₂oz) servings

600g (1lb 5oz) yellow peaches

1. Wash the peaches, remove the stones and slice the fruit.
2. Put the peaches into a saucepan, cover the fruit one-third of the way with water and bring to the boil. Cover and cook over a medium heat for 10 minutes. When done, 3–4 tablespoons of liquid should remain.
3. Blend to obtain a smooth compote.

yummy tips

You can add 1 or 2 fresh mint leaves to the compote when it's finished cooking.

Peaches create a great deal of water. If there's too much liquid left in the saucepan, set it aside. It makes a sweet all-natural syrup you can use instead of sugar as a dessert topping for yogurt or cottage cheese. Try your baby with this sweet treat when they have reached at least 6 months of age.

apple compote
compote de pommes

10 | 15 | 24ʰ | -18°

Makes five 100g (3¹/₂oz) servings

*600g (1lb 5oz) sweet apples
(Gala, Golden Delicious, Fuji)*

1. Wash and peel the apples, remove the cores and any spare pips, then cut the fruit into cubes.
2. Put the apples into a saucepan, cover the fruit halfway with water and bring to the boil. Cook, uncovered, over a medium heat for 15 minutes. When done, 3–4 tablespoons of liquid should remain.
3. Make sure the apples are well cooked before blending them to obtain a smooth compote.

yummy tips

To ring the changes, for babies that are 8 months or older, you can add ½ teaspoon of cinnamon to the apples while they're cooking. My children also love when I add bananas to the apples in this recipe. To do this, replace 2 apples with 2 peeled bananas. Cut the bananas into small slices. Follow the same cooking guidelines and blend. Delicious!

pear compote
compote de poires

🕐	🍲	🗄	❄
7	15	24ʰ	-18°

Makes five 100g (3½oz) servings

*600g (1lb 5oz) pears
(Conference, Williams)*

1. Wash and peel the pears, remove the cores and any spare pips, then cut the fruit into cubes.
2. Put the pears into a saucepan, cover the fruit halfway with water and bring to the boil. Cook, uncovered, over a medium heat for 15 minutes. When done, 3–4 tablespoons of liquid should remain.
3. Make sure the pears are well cooked before blending them to obtain a smooth compote.

yummy tips

This purée tastes even better if you add a vanilla pod while the pears are cooking – try adding this when your baby is 8 months or older. With a knife, open 1 vanilla pod lengthways and scrape it to remove the seeds. Throw the seeds into the saucepan along with the open pod. Before blending, remove the pod. For a caramelised flavour for babies twelve months and over, add 4 tablespoons of clear honey 2–3 minutes before removing the pears from the heat. Stir the honey well once added so it doesn't stick to the saucepan. Blend as described above.

apricot compote
compote d'abricots

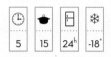

🕐	🍲	🗄	❄
5	15	24ʰ	-18°

Makes five 100g (3½oz) servings

600g (1lb 5oz) apricots

1. Wash and peel the apricots, remove the stones, then cut the flesh into pieces.
2. Put the apricots into a saucepan, cover the fruit halfway with water and bring to the boil. Cover and cook the apricots over a medium heat for 15 minutes. When done, 3–4 tablespoons of liquid should remain.
3. Blend until you have a smooth compote.

yummy tips

Apricots go very well with vanilla – try adding this when your baby is 8 months or older. With a knife, open 1 vanilla pod lengthways and scrape it to remove the seeds. Throw the seeds into the saucepan along with the open pod. Before blending, remove the pod.

Another option: add 2 basil leaves before blending. Try this variation for yourself as an accompaniment to grilled meat or served with goat's cheese.

melon compote
compote de melon

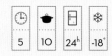

🕐	🍲	🗄	❄
5	10	24ʰ	-18°

Makes five 100g (3½oz) servings

*600g (1lb 5oz) melon
(cantaloupe or other varieties)*

1. Cut the melon in half, remove the seeds, then slice the halves into wedges. Cut away the rind, then slice the fruit into rectangular pieces.
2. Blend for a refreshing no-cook compote.

For a more intense flavour, roast the melon in the oven first. Doing so reduces the amount of water in the fruit and enhances its flavour.
1. Preheat the oven to 200°C (400°F/Gas Mark 6).
2. Follow step 1 in the directions above.
3. Put the melon pieces, without the rind, in a baking dish and cover with foil.
4. Roast in the oven for 20 minutes.
5. Remove the melon from the oven, leave to cool and blend until you have a smooth compote.

yummy tips

Try the roasted version using watermelon. Follow the recipe above, but double the quantity of fruit and make sure you remove all the black seeds. For adults, this compote is an excellent dessert with a scoop of vanilla ice cream and chopped basil leaves.

yellow (mirabelle) plum compote
compote de mirabelles

| 5 | 15 | 24ʰ | -18° |

Makes five 100g (3½oz) servings

750g (1lb 10oz) yellow (Mirabelle) plums

1. Wash the plums and cut them into halves. Remove the stones.
2. Put the plums into a saucepan, cover the fruit halfway with water and bring to the boil. Cover and cook over a low heat for 10–15 minutes.
3. When done, 3–4 tablespoons of liquid should remain. If there's more, you can use it as a natural sweetener to top off dairy desserts. If there's not enough, add a few spoonfuls of water.
4. Blend into a smooth compote.

yummy tips

For babies over twelve months, add 2 tablespoons of clear honey halfway through the cooking time for a sweet snack. For slightly older children, you can sprinkle soft brown sugar in place of honey on the unsweetened compote just before serving for a little crunchiness. If yellow plums are out of season, use frozen plums, which are excellent for making compotes.

mango-banana compote

compote mangues-bananes

⏰	🥘	🗄	❄
5	10	24ʰ	-18˚

Makes five 100g (3½oz) servings

*2 ripe mangoes, about 400g (14oz)
mango flesh
3 bananas*

1. Cut off the sides of the mangoes along either side of the stone. With a small knife, remove the skin from both sides and cut the flesh into pieces. Trim the flesh from around the stone and remove the skin.
2. Remove the banana peels and slice the fruit into small rounds.
3. Put the mango pieces and bananas into a saucepan, cover the fruit halfway with water and bring to the boil. Cover and cook over a low heat for 10 minutes. When done, about 3 tablespoons of liquid will remain.
4. Blend until you have a smooth compote.

yummy tips

Ready-prepared mango (available skinned and sliced) is more practical to use than fresh. Perfect for a compote!

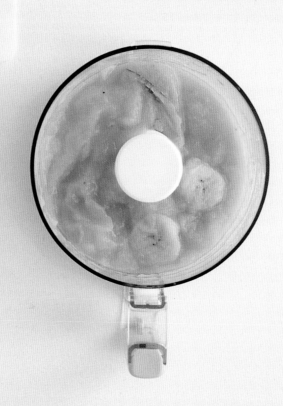

pineapple and lychee compote
compote ananas-litchis

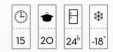

| 15 | 20 | 24ʰ | -18° |

Makes five 100 g (3¹/₂oz) servings

*1 pineapple, about 300g (10¹/₂oz)
pineapple flesh
200g (7oz) lychees, fresh or frozen*

1. Peel the pineapple until every bit of skin has been removed from the fruit. Cut around the hard core to remove it, then cut the flesh of the pineapple into cubes.
2. Peel the lychees if using fresh ones and remove the stones.
3. Put the pineapple and lychees into a saucepan, cover the fruit halfway with water and bring to the boil. Cover and cook over a low heat for 20 minutes. When done cooking, about 3 tablespoons of liquid should remain.
4. Blend until you have a smooth compote.

yummy tips

As this was my daughter's favourite compote when she was little, I made it often. You can freeze pineapple and lychees to use all year round.

cherry and apple compote

compote cerises-pommes

🕐	🍲	🗄	❄
20	15	24^h	-18°

Makes five 100g (3½oz) servings

*About 400g (14oz) cherries
300g (10½oz) apples (Fuji or Golden
Delicious)*

1. Wash the cherries, then remove the stalks and stones with a small knife.
2. Wash and peel the apples, remove the cores and any spare pips, and cut the fruit in cubes.
3. Put the cherries and apples into a saucepan, cover the fruit halfway with water and bring to the boil. Cover and cook over a medium heat for 15 minutes. When done, about 3 tablespoons of liquid should remain.
4. Blend until you have a smooth compote.

yummy tips

Out of season, you can replace the cherries with red grapes. Wash and cut them in half and remove any pips. Use sweet apples (such as Golden Delicious) to balance the slight acidity of the grapes.

plum and pear compote
compote prunes-poires

🕐	🍲	🗄	❄
15	15	24ʰ	-18°

Makes five 100g (3½oz) servings

350g (12oz) plums
*300g (10½oz) sweet pears
(such as Williams)*

1. Wash the plums and remove the stones with a small knife.
2. Wash and peel the pears, remove the cores and any spare pips, and cut the flesh into cubes.
3. Put the plums and pears in a saucepan, cover the fruit one-third of the way with water and bring to the boil. Cover and cook over a medium heat for 15 minutes. When done, about 3 tablespoons of liquid should remain.
4. Blend until you have a smooth compote.

yummy tips
Many different kinds of plums exist, some more acidic than others. Use well-ripened plums. They are sweeter, and their skin will add a slightly sour note.

carrot purée
purée de carottes

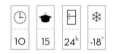

10	15	24ʰ	-18°

Makes five 100g (3½oz) servings

500g (1lb 2oz) carrots
1 teaspoon sunflower oil

1. Wash and peel the carrots, then chop them into small rounds.
2. Put the carrots into a saucepan, cover them with water and bring to the boil. Cover and cook over a medium heat for 15 minutes.
3. Drain the carrots and blend them with the sunflower oil until smooth.

yummy tips

Carrots sometimes lose a little of their sweetness when cooked. To enhance their natural flavour, add a few fresh coriander leaves just before blending (for babies that are at least 6 months old).

For babies that are at least 8 months old, try a Middle Eastern touch: cook the carrots in 200ml (7fl oz) orange juice. After cooking, blend the carrots with the remaining orange juice, ½ teaspoon of ground cumin and, for bébé gourmets over twelve months, a few drops of clear honey. Even grown-ups love it!

broccoli purée
purée de brocolis

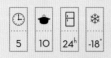

| 5 | 10 | 24ʰ | -18° |

Makes five 100g (3½oz) servings

600g (1lb 5oz) broccoli florets, fresh or frozen
1 teaspoon olive oil

1. Wash the florets if you are using fresh broccoli.
2. Put the broccoli into a saucepan. Cover the broccoli halfway with water, bring to the boil and cook, uncovered, over a medium heat for 10 minutes. When done, about 2 tablespoons of water should remain.
3. Blend the broccoli with the remaining cooking water and the olive oil until smooth.

yummy tips
When Bébé is at least 6 months old, try making this strong-tasting purée sweeter and creamier: add 2 squares of soft cheese just before blending. You can also add a few leaves of fresh flat-leaf parsley or sage before blending.

pea purée
purée de petits pois

⏱	☕	🗄	❄
5	10	24ʰ	-18˚

Makes five 100g
(3¹/₂oz) servings

*500g (1lb 2oz) petits pois or peas,
fresh or frozen
2 tablespoons crème fraîche
(see page 23)*

1. Put the petits pois or peas into a saucepan, cover with water, bring to the boil and cook over a low heat for 7–8 minutes. Drain.
2. Blend with the crème fraîche until you have a smooth purée.

yummy tips

For a mildly tangy note, blend this recipe with 2 fresh mint leaves. This version is excellent for Bébé, as well as the rest of the family, with grilled lamb. Some babies don't like the grainy texture that comes from the peas' somewhat thick skin. Personally, I believe that children should get used to the natural textures of food, but if you need to, you can pass the purée through a fine sieve to acquire a smoother mixture.

green bean purée
purée de haricots verts

Makes five 100g (3½oz) servings

500g (1lb 2oz) green beans, fresh or frozen
1 teaspoon olive oil

1. Trim the ends of the green beans if you are using fresh ones.
2. Put the green beans into a saucepan, cover them halfway with water, bring to the boil, cover and cook over a medium heat for 10 minutes. When done, about 2 tablespoons of water should remain.
3. Blend the green beans with the remaining cooking water and the olive oil until smooth.

yummy tips
You can also make this purée by replacing half the green beans with fresh or frozen peas. The result will be slightly creamier and sweeter than the original recipe. For a taste of summer add 2 fresh basil leaves before blending either version of this recipe.

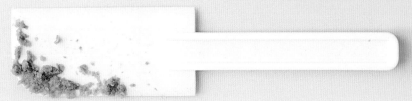

avocado purée
purée d'avocat

5 | 5

Makes one 100g
(3½oz) serving

1 ripe avocado
2–3 drops lemon juice

1. Cut open the avocado and remove the stone.
2. Scoop out the avocado flesh with a spoon and put it into a bowl.
3. Mash the flesh with the lemon juice (to preserve the green colour) until you have a smooth purée.

yummy tips

Unlike other fruits, avocados ripen once picked, not on the tree. A hard avocado is therefore a sign of freshness! To ripen them, simply leave at room temperature in a brown paper bag. To speed the process, place a banana or apple in the bag along with the avocado.

My daughter Maya still devours this purée with chicken, grilled meat or fish such as tuna or swordfish. Now that she's a few years older, we add a pinch of sea salt and a drop of Tabasco to her 'kiddie guacamole'.

sweet potato purée
purée de patates douces

5   15   24ʰ   -18°

Makes five 100g
(3½oz) servings

600g (1lb 5oz) sweet potatoes
10g (¼oz) butter
(see page 23)

1. Wash and peel the sweet potatoes, then cut them into cubes.
2. Put the cubes into a saucepan, cover them with water, bring to the boil and cook over a medium heat for 15 minutes. Drain.
3. Blend with the butter until you have a smooth purée.

yummy tips
Sweet potatoes are a favourite with kids. For older babies I often cut the sweet potatoes into *batons* (chips) and roast them in the oven for about 20 minutes. The flavour becomes even more pronounced, and kids love to eat with their fingers!

parsnip purée
purée de panais

| 10 | 15 | 24ʰ | -18˚ |

Makes five 100g (3½oz) servings

600g (1lb 5oz) parsnips
200ml (7fl oz) full-fat milk
(see page 23)
10g (¼oz) butter

1. Wash and peel the parsnips, then cut them into cubes.
2. Put the cubes into a saucepan, cover with milk, bring the milk to the boil, stirring constantly, then lower heat, cover and cook over a medium heat for 15 minutes. Drain, keeping a bit of the drained milk aside.
3. Blend with the butter and a little of the cooking milk until you have a smooth, creamy purée.

yummy tips

You can vary this recipe by replacing 1 parsnip with a sweet apple (Fuji or similar). Add the peeled, cored and cubed apples 5 minutes before the end of the cooking time. Drain the excess milk so that the purée is not too wet, then blend. This purée is sweeter and fruitier than most, so it's great for even the smallest babies. I serve it with beef bourguignon or lamb steaks to older children.

cauliflower purée
purée de chou-fleur

⏱	🍲	🗄	❄
5	15	24ʰ	-18°

Makes five 100g (3½oz) servings

600g (1lb 5oz) cauliflower florets, fresh or frozen
200ml (7fl oz) full-fat milk (see page 23)
10g (¼oz) butter

1. Wash the cauliflower florets if you are using fresh.
2. In a saucepan, bring the milk to the boil, add the cauliflower and cook over a medium heat for 15 minutes (be careful, as the milk can boil over easily).
3. Drain off the milk and set aside.
4. Blend the cauliflower with the butter, adding a little of the cooking milk until you have a smooth, creamy purée.

yummy tips

Add a sprig of fresh thyme 5 minutes before the end of the cooking time and remove the sprig before blending. The thyme will add sweetness without overpowering the taste of the cauliflower.

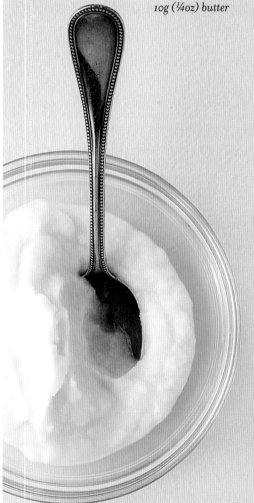

pumpkin purée
purée de potiron

10 | 15 | 24ʰ | -18°

Makes five 100 g (3½oz) servings

750g (1lb 10oz) pumpkin or
butternut squash
1 large waxy potato
10g (¼oz) butter
(see page 23)
2—3 drops lemon juice

1. Wash and peel the pumpkin or squash and potato. Deseed the pumpkin and cut the vegetables into small cubes. It will seem like a lot of pumpkin, but pumpkin loses a lot of water when it cooks.
2. Put the cubes into a saucepan, cover them with water, bring to the boil and cook over a medium heat for 15 minutes. Drain.
3. Blend the vegetable mixture with the butter and lemon juice until you have a smooth purée.

yummy tips

The taste of pumpkin can sometimes be a bit earthy. The lemon juice adds the touch of acidity needed for balance while bringing out the pumpkin's natural taste.

This purée is even better with a pinch of ground cumin or some fresh vanilla – try this when your baby is at least 8 months old . If you opt for cumin, add ¼ teaspoon ground cumin before blending. For the vanilla, slice open a pod, scrape out the seeds with a knife and add the seeds to the pumpkin and potato just before blending.

potato and sweetcorn purée
purée de maïs et pommes de terre

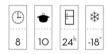

8 | 10 | 24ʰ | -18°

Makes five 100g (3¹/₂oz) servings

450g (about 1lb) potatoes
400g (14oz) sweetcorn,
frozen or tinned
10g (¹/₄oz) butter
(see page 23)

1. Wash and peel the potatoes, then cut them into cubes.
2. Put the cubes into a saucepan, cover them with water and bring to the boil.
3. Add the sweetcorn and cook the vegetables over a medium heat for 10 minutes. Drain.
4. Blend the vegetable mixture with the butter until you have a smooth purée.

yummy tips

For a change, use carrots instead of potatoes. As with peas, the sweetcorn skin creates a slightly grainy purée. If Bébé doesn't like it, pass the purée through a fine sieve before serving.

Milo, 7 months, tester

first lunches

&

first sweets

moving on – over 6 months

Dr Jean Lalau Keraly, paediatric nutritionist and endocrinologist

In just a few months, your baby has adjusted to a new diet. Now she is starting to eat real portions of vegetables or fruit, even though breast milk or formula is still her main food source. She's becoming more independent, and may even be starting to feed herself – or enjoy playing – with her own spoon. In the evening she delights in her breast milk or formula, maybe alongside a bit of cereal, depending on her appetite.

Introduction of new foods

From 6 months, your baby can take another step on the path to eating like a grown-up: you can introduce meat, fish, cereals, cheese and other dairy products besides breast milk or formula into her diet. The arrival of these new foods means parents can offer more interesting recipes and elaborate choices. It also means they can begin to mesh Baby's meals with the family's, delighting the baby because such a move indicates that her social status in the family has risen. It's fun for the parents as it makes for simpler meal logistics.

Ever so slowly

If you have introduced meat into the diet of your six- or seven-month-old baby, make sure you don't turn her into a first-class carnivore! At this age, 20g (¾oz), or about 2 teaspoons, a day of animal protein will do for her body. You can serve up to 30g (1oz), or 1 tablespoon, at this time if your baby seems to be a big fan. This is the time to serve your mini-gourmet more elaborate lunches with mixed meat or fish, along with a side dish, so Baby can differentiate the textures, colours and flavours of the food. The meal naturally ends with a sweet touch – a small serving of fruit compote or crushed fruit – and why not mix in some fromage frais or natural, unsweetened Greek yogurt?

Respect your baby's appetite, desires and preferences

If she doesn't finish eating, don't force her. If she wants more vegetables, give her some. Unlike we adults, who are capable of serving ourselves three helpings of Aunt Monica's lasagna – with extra sauce, please, Auntie! – your baby knows how to listen to her body when she's eaten enough. If she's no longer hungry, she'll refuse pudding (even if that seems inconceivable to you). If she doesn't like the sweetcorn compote that you lovingly prepared, don't take it personally. You can have her try it again some other time. She has the right, just as you do, not to like certain foods and her tastes will evolve. The simple rule is just to have her taste.

At 7 months
Your baby can start eating eggs. I would suggest only serving the egg yolk, however, as the white can be allergenic . Start by offering half of the yolk (well cooked).

At 8 months
You can let your baby chew on a crust of bread, which will help with teething. Always sit next to your little one as she nibbles her bread. If she bites off a piece that's too big, she won't be able to spit it out herself. If you're worried about an accident, try rice cakes instead. They are just as pleasurable for the baby but are safer because the rice grains break off as the child chews. You can also introduce spices and vanilla cautiously to your baby's diet, for extra flavour.

In this chapter
You are going to discover real lunches that mark a new era of tasty discoveries for your baby. This is the time of flavour association and more complex recipes that are bolder than before. As your baby's taste buds awaken, you will teach her how to accept and appreciate new things, a talent she will carry late into life. She will not become the kind of person who relies solely on starchy staple foods like rice and pasta.

chicken with carrots and apricots

poulet aux carottes et abricots

🕐 15 🍲 20 🗄 24ʰ ❄ -18°

Makes five 100g (3½oz) servings

600g (1lb 5oz) carrots
300g (10½oz) apricots, fresh or frozen
1 chicken breast, about 100g (3½oz)
1 teaspoon sunflower oil
2 teaspoons finely chopped shallots
200ml (7fl oz) orange juice

1. Wash and peel the carrots, then cut them into rounds.
2. Wash and stone the apricots.
3. Cut the chicken breast into small pieces.
4. In a heavy-based saucepan, heat the oil over a medium heat and add the shallots. Brown them for 1–2 minutes, then add the chicken breast pieces.
5. Once the chicken pieces are browned on all sides, add the carrots, apricots and orange juice. Add water to cover the mixture halfway.
6. Bring to the boil, reduce the heat, cover and leave to simmer for 15–20 minutes. Check to make sure the carrots are tender before removing from the heat.
7. Blend to a smooth purée.

accompaniments

Serve this dish with Parsnip Purée (page 43), Turnip Purée (page 68) or Pea Purée (page 39).

yummy tips

You can replace the fresh or frozen fruit with 10 ready-to-eat dried apricots, but you will need to double the amount of orange juice used. Not only are dried apricots easily found in stores year-round, they also are a valuable source of iron and B vitamins.

chicken and tarragon fricassee
fricassée de poulet à l'estragon

🕐	🍲	🗄	❄
15	15	24ʰ	-18°

Makes five 100g (3½oz) servings

100g (3½oz) turnip
115g (4oz) courgettes
100g (3½oz) broccoli florets
85g (3oz) green beans
1 chicken breast, about 100g (3½oz)
1 teaspoon sunflower oil
4 tablespoons low-salt vegetable stock
2 teaspoons chopped fresh tarragon

1. Wash the vegetables and peel the turnips and courgettes.
2. Cut the turnips into cubes and the courgettes into rounds.
3. Cut the chicken breast into pieces.
4. In a heavy-based saucepan, heat the oil over a medium heat and brown the pieces of chicken. Add the vegetables, stock and tarragon, then cover the ingredients halfway with water and bring to the boil. Cook over a medium heat for 10 minutes.
5. Remove from the heat and drain, reserving some of the cooking liquid. Blend until you have a smooth purée. Add a little of the cooking liquid if the mixture is too dense or grainy.

accompaniments
Serve this dish with Sweet Potato Purée (page 42) or Carrot and Cumin Purée (page 67).

yummy tips
Want to show off for the whole family? Turn this recipe into Chicken Stuffed with Tarragon and Prosciutto. Count on 150g (5oz) of chicken breast per person. Cut an opening in each breast at its thickest point, making a pocket without cutting the chicken completely in two. Cook the vegetables with the tarragon according to the recipe above, drain and blend to make a dense purée. Place each chicken breast on a slice of prosciutto, then spoon some vegetable purée into the opening. Roll the breast to close the pocket and wrap the ham around the chicken, securing it with a couple of cocktail sticks. Preheat the oven to 200°C (400°F/Gas Mark 6) and bake for 10–12 minutes. Remove the cocktail sticks and cut the chicken in two to reveal the pretty stuffing. Serve with a mixed green salad and bread spread with fresh goat's cheese.

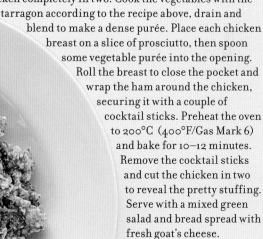

turkey with sweetcorn and onions
dinde au maïs et aux oignons doux

5   20   24ʰ   -18°

Makes five 100g (3½oz) servings

1 turkey escalope, about 100g (3½oz)
2 teaspoons sunflower oil
2 tablespoons finely chopped mild onion
350g (12oz) sweetcorn,
frozen or canned

1. Cut the turkey escalope into small pieces.
2. In a heavy-based saucepan, heat the oil over a medium heat, add the onions and cook for 1 minute. Add the turkey pieces and brown them on all sides while stirring non-stop. Add the sweetcorn, mix well and cover the mixture halfway with water.
3. Bring to the boil, reduce the heat, cover and leave to simmer over a low heat for 15 minutes.
4. Remove from the heat and blend until you have a smooth purée.
5. If the texture is too grainy, add a few spoonfuls of water and blend to your desired consistency.

accompaniments
Serve this dish with Mashed Pumpkin and Apple (page 66) or Sweet Potato Purée (page 42).

yummy tips
Transform this recipe into a risotto for the whole family: fry 100g (3½oz) of Arborio rice with the onions and sunflower oil. Add just over 125ml (4fl oz) of water, 125ml (4fl oz) of low-salt chicken stock and the sweetcorn. Stir regularly until the water is absorbed and the rice is tender. In a frying pan, brown the turkey pieces (about 70g/2½oz per person) in 2 teaspoons of sunflower oil and 2 teaspoons lemon juice. When the rice is cooked, add 50g (1¾oz) grated Parmesan, 10g (¼oz) butter and 5 chopped fresh sage leaves. Before serving, mix the turkey into the risotto.

turkey with chestnuts and apples
dinde aux marrons et pommes

Makes five 100g (3½oz) servings

400g (14oz) apples
1 turkey escalope, about 100g (3½oz)
2 teaspoons finely chopped shallots
1 teaspoon sunflower oil
½ teaspoon cinnamon (see page 51)
½ teaspoon freshly grated ginger
½ teaspoon cloves
200g (7oz) pre-cooked chestnuts

1. Wash and peel the apples, remove the cores and any spare pips and cut the fruit into pieces.
2. Cut the turkey escalope into pieces, then brown it in a saucepan over a medium heat with the shallots and sunflower oil.
3. Add the spices, stirring with the turkey pieces for about one minute to distribute, then add the apples and chestnuts. Fill the pan halfway with water, bring to the boil and lower the heat. Cover and simmer for 15 minutes.
4. Remove from the heat. Blend until you have a smooth purée.

accompaniments
Serve this dish with Sweet Potato Purée (page 42) or Carrot and Cumin Purée (page 67).

yummy tips
Want to prepare this recipe for family members who are one year and over? Child's play! Count on 150g (5oz) of turkey escalope per person. Preheat the oven to 200°C (400°F/ Gas Mark 6). Place the turkey in an ovenproof dish, combine a few drops of orange juice and low-sodium soy sauce, then brush the turkey with the mixture. Bake for 12–15 minutes. Serve with a side dish of sautéed chestnuts and apples, preparing them as you would for the recipe above but without adding water (sauté at a medium heat and caramelise in the liquid released from the apples).

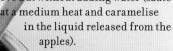

orange veal piccata
piccata de veau à l'orange

10 15 24ʰ -18°

Makes five 100g (3½oz) servings

175g (6oz) carrots
250g (8oz) fennel bulb
1 veal escalope, about 100g (3½oz)
1 teaspoon sunflower oil
1 teaspoon finely chopped shallots
300ml (10fl oz) orange juice

1. Wash and peel the carrots, then cut them into rounds. Wash the fennel, then remove the stalks and cut the bulb into thin strips. Cut the veal into cubes.
2. In a heavy-based saucepan, heat the oil over a medium heat, add the shallots and the cubes of veal and brown them on all sides.
3. Add the carrots, fennel and orange juice. Cook, uncovered, over a medium heat for 12 minutes, making sure there is enough orange juice in the pan. If not, add a few tablespoons of juice or water to get the right quantity. Turn down the heat or cover the pan if you notice the liquid is evaporating too quickly.
4. Remove from the heat and blend until you have a smooth purée.

accompaniments
Serve this dish with Parsnip Purée (page 43) or Pea Purée (page 39).

yummy tips
For bigger kids, I serve a veal escalope, seared for 3 minutes on each side and seasoned with a tiny pinch of sea salt and several drops of lemon juice. This is accompanied by the carrot, fennel and orange purée. For the purée, cook the carrots and fennel in orange juice as directed above, then blend.

veal stew with 'forgotten' vegetables
mijoté de veau aux légumes oubliés

⏰	🍲	🗄	❄
15	20	24ʰ	-18°

Makes five 100g (3½oz) servings

200g (7oz) swede
100g (3½oz) parsnips
55g (2oz) celeriac
55g (2oz) fennel bulb
1 veal escalope, about 100g (3½oz)
1 teaspoon sunflower oil
2 teaspoons finely chopped shallots

1. Wash and peel the swede, parsnips and celeriac. Wash the fennel and remove the stalks.
2. Cut the vegetables into pieces and cut the veal escalope into cubes.
3. In a saucepan, heat the oil over a medium heat, add the shallots and the cubes of veal and brown the cubes on all sides. Add the vegetables, cover them halfway with water and bring to the boil. Reduce the heat, cover the pan and simmer for 20 minutes. There should be about 3 tablespoons of liquid left in the pan after cooking.
4. Remove from the heat and blend until you have a smooth purée.

accompaniments
Serve this dish with Green Bean Purée (page 40), Broccoli Purée (page 38) or Pea Purée (page 39).

yummy tips
For bigger kids, brown the veal pieces with the chopped shallots and set aside. Cook the vegetables according to the recipe and blend only the vegetables to make a purée. Serve with whole green beans, broccoli or peas.

lamb stew with green vegetables
petit navarin d'agneau aux légumes verts

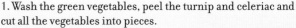

10	25	24ʰ	-18°

Makes five 100g (3½oz) servings

55g (2oz) courgettes
75g (2¾oz) green beans
50g (1¾oz) broccoli florets
75g (2¾oz) peas, fresh or frozen
100g (3½oz) turnip
30g (1oz) celeriac
1 teaspoon sunflower oil
100g (3½oz) lamb shoulder or leg, cut into small pieces

1. Wash the green vegetables, peel the turnip and celeriac and cut all the vegetables into pieces.
2. In a heavy-based saucepan, heat the oil over a medium heat and brown the lamb. Add the turnip and celeriac, cover the mixture halfway with water and bring to the boil. Reduce the heat, cover and simmer for 15 minutes.
3. Add the green vegetables and cook for another 10 minutes. About 3 tablespoons of liquid should be left in the pan at the end of cooking. If not, pour some out or add a little water to get the right quantity.
4. Remove from the heat. Blend until you have a smooth purée.

accompaniments
Serve this dish with Cauliflower Purée (page 44) or Carrot and Cumin Purée (page 67).

yummy tips
For a family of four, use 100g (3½oz) of lamb per person and double the remaining quantities in the recipe. When you add the turnip and celeriac, also add 250ml (8fl oz) low-salt chicken stock, 1 crushed garlic clove and 1 teaspoon chopped fresh thyme. Before serving, season with sea salt and freshly ground pepper to taste.

Italian beef ragout
ragoût de boeuf à l'italienne

⏱	🍲	🗄	❄
10	25	24ʰ	-18°

Makes five 100g (3½oz) servings

200g (7oz) tomatoes
115g (4oz) courgettes
1 celery stick
55g (2oz) carrot
100g (3½oz) stewing beef (neck or shoulder)
1 teaspoon olive oil
½ garlic clove, chopped
2 teaspoons tomato purée
½ teaspoon chopped fresh thyme
125ml (4fl oz) water

1. Wash the vegetables and peel the carrot. Dice the vegetables and cut the meat into small pieces.
2. In a heavy-based saucepan, heat the olive oil over a medium heat and brown the garlic and beef. Add the vegetables, tomato purée, thyme and water. Cover and simmer for 25 minutes.
3. Remove from the heat and blend until the ragout has a smooth texture.

accompaniments
Serve with Parsnip Purée (page 43) or Avocado Purée (page 41).

yummy tips
This dish is equally delicious served over pasta. If you decide to try it this way, consider serving it with additional green vegetables such as green beans.

mini-flan with sweet potato and cod
petit flan de patate douce et cabillaud

10	20	24ʰ	-18˚

Makes five 100g (3½oz) servings

300g (10½oz) sweet potato
100g (3½oz) potato
1 cod fillet, about 150g (5oz)
10g (¼oz) butter
2 fresh sage leaves, finely chopped

1. Wash and peel the potatoes, then cut them into cubes. Put the cubes into a saucepan, cover them with water and bring to the boil. Reduce the heat, cover and cook for 15 minutes.
2. Make sure there are no bones in the fish.
3. In a separate saucepan, let the fish fillet simmer in boiling water for 5 minutes.
4. Remove the potatoes from the heat and drain, then add the butter and mash until you have a smooth purée.
5. Finely chop the cod and blend with the purée and the sage. Using a ramekin or cooking ring, make the shape of a flan in the middle of Bébé's plate.

accompaniments
Serve this dish with Pea Purée (page 42), Broccoli Purée (page 38) or Green Bean Purée (page 40).

yummy tips
The rest of the family can enjoy this dish on a cold winter's night as well. Count on 150g (5oz) of cod fillet per person. Put the fillets into an ovenproof dish, add a few teaspoons of olive oil, a few drops of lemon juice and a pinch of sea salt. Cover with the sweet potato and potato purée. Preheat the oven to 200°C (400°F/Gas Mark 6) and bake for 15 minutes.

salmon with spinach
saumon aux épinards

🕐	🍲	📅	❄
5	15	24ʰ	-18°

Makes five 100g
(3½oz) servings

1 salmon fillet, about 100g (3½oz)
1 teaspoon lemon juice
500g (1lb 2oz) frozen spinach
4 tablespoons low-salt vegetable stock
2 tablespoons crème fraîche

1. Make sure there are no bones in the salmon fillet and cut it into small cubes.
2. Put the salmon cubes on a plate and sprinkle them with the lemon juice. Set aside.
3. Put the spinach into a saucepan with the vegetable stock and add water until the spinach is just covered. Bring to the boil. Cover and cook over a medium heat for 10 minutes. Add the salmon cubes and cook for 5 minutes more.
4. Drain the mixture and put back on the heat in the saucepan. Add the crème fraîche, mix well and allow to heat through.
5. Blend until you have a smooth purée.

accompaniments
Serve this dish with Old-Fashioned Mashed Potatoes (page 68) or Turnip Purée (page 68).

yummy tips
This dish will work just as well with white fish such as cod or sole. In that case omit the lemon juice, because it tends to overpower the more delicate flavour of white fish.

sole with courgettes and broad beans
sole aux courgettes et aux fèves

🕐	🍲	📋	❄
10	15	24ʰ	-18°

Makes five 100g (3½oz) servings

*3 to 4 fillets of sole,
around 100g (3½oz) each
175g (6oz) courgettes
150g (5½oz) broad beans,
fresh or frozen
1 teaspoon olive oil
½ garlic clove, crushed
2 teaspoons finely chopped shallots*

1. Make sure there are no bones in the fish.
2. Wash the courgettes, then cut them into rounds. Shell and peel the broad beans if using fresh.
3. Heat the olive olive oil in a saucepan over a medium heat and brown the garlic and shallots. Add the courgettes and broad beans, cover them halfway with water and bring to the boil. Cook for about 8 minutes.
4. Place the sole fillets on top of the vegetable mixture, cover and cook for a further 2–3 minutes.
5. Remove from the heat. When done cooking, 2–3 tablespoons of cooking liquid should remain at the base of the saucepan. If not, pour some out or add a little water to get the right quantity.
6. Blend until you have a smooth purée.

accompaniments

Serve this dish with Sweet Potato Purée (page 42), Carrot and Cumin Purée (page 67) or Mashed Pumpkin and Apple (page 66).

yummy tips

If you can't find broad beans, replace them with peas. This recipe can easily be adapted to feed the whole family. Use the ingredients to make an appetising *parmentier de poisson* (fish pie) with sweet potato topping. Place the courgettes, broad beans, garlic, shallots, a few drops of lemon juice and some basil in a casserole dish. Place the raw sole fillets (allow two to three per person according to their size) on top of the vegetables and cover with a layer of mashed sweet potatoes. Preheat the oven to 200°C (400°F/Gas Mark 6) and bake for 20 minutes. Voilà!

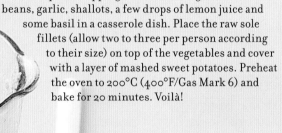

sea bass with fennel and green grapes

bar au fenouil et aux raisins blancs

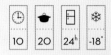

🕐	🍲	🗄	❄
10	20	24ʰ	-18°

Makes five 100g (3½oz) servings

150g (5½oz) fennel bulb
100g (3½oz) seedless green grapes
or 55g (2oz) sultanas
55g (2oz) carrot
55g (2oz) parsnip or waxy potatoes
1 sea bass or tilapia (or other mild-flavoured white fish) fillet, about 100g (3½oz)
1 teaspoon sunflower oil
200ml (7fl oz) orange juice

1. Wash the fennel, remove the stalks and cut the bulb into thin slices. Wash and peel the carrot and the parsnip, then dice them.
2. Make sure the sea bass fillet has no bones.
3. In a heavy-based saucepan, heat the oil over a medium heat and brown the fennel slices. Add the grapes, carrot and parsnip. Pour in the orange juice and bring to the boil. Lower the heat, cover and simmer for 15 minutes.
4. Place the sea bass fillet on top of the vegetables, cover and cook for a further 5–6 minutes.
5. Remove from heat. When done cooking, about 3 tablespoons of juice should remain. If not, pour some juice out or add a little water to get the right quantity.
6. Blend until you have a smooth purée.

accompaniments
Serve this dish with Carrot Coriander Purée (page 67) or Sweet Potato Purée (page 42).

yummy tips

For an adult dinner, stuff whole sea bass bellies with fennel and lemon slices. Preheat the oven to 180°C (350°F/Gas Mark 4) and bake for 25 minutes. Serve the fillets over wild rice with fennel and raisins. To prepare the wild rice, brown the fennel slices and the grapes or sultanas in a little sunflower oil. Add 100g (3½oz) rice and stir until the rice is slightly translucent. Add 300ml (10fl oz) of water and a pinch of salt. Cover and cook until the water is completely absorbed.

tuna Niçoise
thon à la Niçoise

10   15   24ʰ   -18˚

Makes five 100g (3½oz) servings

115g (4oz) courgettes
200g (7oz) tomatoes
55g (2oz) aubergine
1 fresh or frozen tuna steak,
about 100g (3½oz)
2 teaspoons olive oil
½ clove garlic, chopped
1 tablespoon tomato purée
½ teaspoon dried thyme
125ml (4 fl oz) water

1. Wash the vegetables and cut them into cubes.
2. Cut the tuna into cubes.
3. In a heavy-based saucepan, heat the olive oil over a medium heat and brown the garlic and tuna cubes. Add the vegetables, tomato purée and thyme. Pour in the water and bring to the boil. Lower the heat, cover and simmer for 15 minutes.
4. Remove from the heat and blend until you have a smooth purée.

accompaniments
This dish goes nicely with Parmesan Polenta (page 69) or Fine Semolina with Thyme (page 69).

yummy tips
If you find the aubergine has added a bitter note to the dish, simply add 1 tablespoon of tomato ketchup – its sugar will neutralise the bitter taste. For a family meal, sear or grill tuna steaks (150g/5oz per person) until they're pink in the middle (about 4 minutes on each side). Prepare the vegetables with tomato purée, thyme and 125ml (4fl oz) water according to the recipe and add a pinch of salt. Serve the steaks topped with these mixed vegetables and one of the accompaniments mentioned above.

mashed pumpkin and apple
purée de potiron et de pommes

10 15

24ʰ -18°

Makes five 100g
(3½oz) servings

500g (1lb 2oz) pumpkin or
butternut squash
200g (7oz) sweet-tart apples
(Gala, Fuji)
200g (7oz) waxy potato
10g (¼oz) butter
2 drops lemon juice

1. Wash and peel the pumpkin or squash, apples and potato. Deseed the pumpkin, remove the apples' cores and any spare pips and cut everything into cubes.
2. Put the cubes into a saucepan, cover with water and bring to the boil. Cook for 15 minutes. Remove from the heat and drain.
3. Blend the cooked fruit and veggies with the butter and lemon juice until you have a smooth purée.

pumpkin purée with cumin
purée de potiron au cumin

10 15

24ʰ -18°

Makes five 100g
(3½oz) servings

750g (1lb 10oz) pumpkin or
butternut squash
200g (7oz) waxy potato
10g (¼oz) butter
2–3 drops lemon juice
½–1 teaspoon ground cumin, to taste
(see page 51)

1. Wash and peel the pumpkin or squash and potato. Deseed the pumpkin and cut the vegetables into small cubes.
2. Put the cubes into a saucepan, cover with water and bring to the boil. Cook for 15 minutes. Remove from the heat and drain.
3. Blend the vegetables with the butter, lemon juice and cumin until you have a smooth purée.

carrot and cumin purée
purée de carottes au cumin

5 | 15

24ʰ | -18°

Makes five 100g
(3½oz) servings

400g (14oz) carrots
1 teaspoon sunflower oil
1 teaspoon lemon juice
Pinch of ground cumin (see page 51)
125ml (4fl oz) water

1. Wash and peel the carrots, then cut them into rounds.
2. In a heavy-based saucepan, heat the oil and sauté the carrots over a medium heat for 5 minutes. Add the lemon juice, cumin and water. Cook for a further 10 minutes. When done, the water should be completely absorbed and the carrots tender.
3. Blend until you have a smooth purée.

carrot-coriander purée
purée de carottes à la coriandre

5 | 15

24ʰ | -18°

Makes five 100g
(3½oz) servings

500g (1lb 2oz) carrots
4 fresh coriander leaves, chopped
1 teaspoon sunflower oil

1. Wash and peel the carrots, then cut them into rounds.
2. Put the carrots into a saucepan, cover them with water, bring to the boil and cook for 15 minutes. Remove from the heat and drain.
3. Blend the carrots with the coriander and sunflower oil until you have a smooth purée.

turnip purée
purée de navets

5 | 15

24ʰ | -18°

Makes five 100g
(3½oz) servings

500g (1lb 2oz) turnips
10g (¼oz) butter

1. Wash and peel the turnips, then cut them into small pieces.
2. Put the turnips into a saucepan, cover them with water, bring to the boil and cook for 15 minutes. Remove from the heat and drain.
3. Blend the turnips with the butter until you have a smooth purée.

old-fashioned mashed potatoes
purée de pommes de terre à l'ancienne

5 | 15

24ʰ | -18°

Makes five 100g
(3½oz) servings

400g (14oz) potatoes
100ml (3½fl oz) full-fat milk
10g (¼oz) butter

1. Wash and peel the potatoes, then cut them into small pieces.
2. Put the potatoes into a saucepan, cover them with water, bring to the boil and cook for 15 minutes. Remove from the heat and drain.
3. Use a potato ricer to mash the potatoes with the milk and butter (never blend potatoes, unless you want to make an inedible potato paste).

Parmesan polenta
polenta au parmesan

Makes one 100g
(3½oz) serving

100ml (3½fl oz) full-fat milk
2 tablespoons grated Parmesan
1½ tablespoons dried polenta

1. Bring the milk to the boil with the Parmesan,
stirring constantly over a medium heat.
2. Remove from the heat, toss in the polenta and
stir vigorously.
3. Continue to stir until the polenta is creamy and
uniform in texture. Serve immediately.

fine semolina with thyme
semoule fine au thym

Makes one 100g
(3½oz) serving

4 tablespoons water
Pinch of dried thyme
50g (1¾oz) fine semolina

1. Bring the water to the boil with the thyme.
2. Remove the saucepan from the heat and add the
semolina. Cover the saucepan and leave the semolina
to expand for 5 minutes.
3. Fluff the semolina with a fork before serving.

fruit coulis
coulis de fruits

Fruit coulis makes a great quick pudding that can be combined with natural yogurt or fromage frais, depending on what you have in your refrigerator and what Bébé is craving. It's up to you to create your own dessert, mixing and matching the fruit coulis proposed in the following section. And you're not allowed to steal Bébé's dessert!

cherry coulis
coulis de cerises

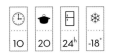

Makes five 100g
(3½oz) servings

*600g (1lb 5oz) cherries
2–3 tablespoons water*

1. Wash the cherries and remove the stones.
2. Put the cherries into a saucepan and crush them lightly with your hand or a fork, so they release a bit of their juice. Cook them over a low heat for 20 minutes. Add water as needed if the fruit does not provide enough liquid.
3. Remove from the heat and blend to a smooth coulis.

yummy tips
You and your partner can eat this coulis on top of a panna cotta or with a slice of mature cheese (such as Comté).

blueberry coulis
coulis de myrtilles

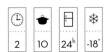

Makes five 100g
(3½oz) servings

*500g (1lb 2oz) blueberries,
fresh or frozen
2–3 tablespoons water*

1. Wash the blueberries.
2. Put the blueberries into a saucepan and crush them lightly with your hand or a fork, so they release a bit of their juice. Cook them over a very low heat for 10 minutes. Add water as needed if the fruit does not provide enough liquid.
3. Remove from the heat and blend to a smooth coulis.

yummy tips
Blueberry stains are very difficult to remove. The little bib Bébé usually wears will not be enough to protect that lovely pullover granny gave him! But don't let that danger deprive Bébé of this delicious fruit. Simply dress him in a bigger bib!

raspberry–brown sugar coulis

coulis de framboises et cassonade

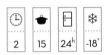

Makes five 100g
(3½oz) servings

*500g (1lb 2oz) raspberries,
fresh or frozen*
1 tablespoon soft brown sugar
*2 tablespoons water (if you're using
frozen fruit, don't add water)*

1. Wash the raspberries well.
2. Put them into a saucepan and crush them lightly with your hand or a fork, so they release a bit of their juice. Add the soft brown sugar and water, then cook them over a low heat for 15 minutes. If the mixture appears dry to you, add water as needed.
3. Remove from the heat and blend to a smooth coulis.

yummy tips

Raspberries are naturally acidic, which is why this recipe contains a bit of sugar. For bigger kids – and a crunch – you can add the soft brown sugar at the end of the cooking time. The sugar crystals won't melt and the coulis will be a bit crunchy.

strawberry-mint coulis

coulis de fraises à la menthe

Makes five 100g
(3½oz) servings

500g (1lb 2oz) strawberries
3 tablespoons water
4 fresh mint leaves

1. Wash the strawberries well and remove any stalks.
2. Put the strawberries into a saucepan and crush them lightly with your hand or a fork, so they release a bit of their juice. Add the water and cook the berries over a low heat for 15 minutes.
3. Add the mint leaves and cook for a further 5 minutes. If the mixture appears dry to you, add water as needed.
4. Remove from the heat and blend to a smooth coulis.

yummy tips

In early summer, when strawberries are the sweetest, I serve this coulis to adults with vanilla ice cream. I always make extra strawberry coulis and freeze it, so I can take it out in winter and serve it over chocolate fondant (*fondant au chocolat*).

nectarine coulis
coulis de nectarines

5	10	24ʰ	-18°

Makes five 100g (3½oz) servings

500g (1lb 2oz) nectarines
4 tablespoons water

1. Peel the nectarines, cut the flesh into pieces and throw away the stones.
2. Put the nectarine pieces into a saucepan and crush them lightly with your hand or a fork, so they release a bit of their juice. Add the water and cook the nectarines over a low heat for 10 minutes. If the mixture appears dry to you, add water as needed.
3. Remove from the heat and blend to a smooth coulis.

yummy tips
Nectarines are easier to peel than peaches, but you can also prepare this coulis with the latter.

mango coulis
coulis de mangue

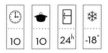

10	10	24ʰ	-18°

Makes five 100g (3½oz) servings

500g (1lb 2oz) mangoes
4 tablespoons water

1. Cut off the sides of the mangoes along either side of the stone. Cut the sides into several half-moons and remove the skin. Trim the flesh from around the stones and remove the skin.
2. Put the mango pieces into a saucepan and crush them lightly with your hand or a fork, so they release a bit of their juice. Add the water and cook them over a low heat for 10 minutes. If the mixture appears dry to you, add water as needed.
3. Remove from the heat and blend to a smooth coulis.

yummy tips
Prepare the mangoes ahead of time and freeze for when you are short on time.

raw, pulpy and blended fruits
les crus, pulpes et mixes

All of the following fruits can be blended or crushed raw and served to Bébé. It's best to prepare and serve them on the spot, as they contain too much water to withstand the freezing process. Serve them with yogurt or, if Bébé has learnt to chew, a soft cake or biscuit.

Once Bébé has acquired a taste for raw fruit and can manage finger foods, feel free to serve her these raw fruits in large pieces that she can eat with her own fingers.

melon

Cut the melon into slices and remove the skin and seeds. Blend.

peach

Cut the flesh from the stone and, using a knife, take the skin off the flesh. Blend.

mango

Cut off the sides of the mango along either side of the stone. Cut these sides into several half-moons and remove the skin. Trim the flesh from around the stone and remove the skin. Blend.

watermelon

Cut the melon into pieces and remove the rind and seeds. Blend.

clementine pulp with a hint of cinnamon

Peel the clementine and divide it into segments. Using a knife, cut each segment lengthways and separate the pulp from the thin skin. Remove any pips. Crush the pulp with a fork. Do not blend, unless you want juice! Mix in a dash of cinnamon.

Vera, 16 months, foodie

first dinners

from 9 months

Dr Jean Lalau Keraly, paediatric nutritionist and endocrinologist

From nine months, your little one is no longer a baby but not a big kid, either. At this age, he can discover dishes composed of mashed vegetables and starches, served alongside small portions of protein, and he may be eating larger portions at lunchtimes. Even though the list of foods he can eat has become longer, you still need to feed him sensibly, without pressure to grow up too quickly. His body is still fragile and there will be plenty of time for him to try Aunt Petra's pickled onions later, when his stomach is able to digest it properly.

Choose foods wisely
Now you'll be preparing dinner based on foods kids tend to love: rice, pasta, polenta. These starches do a suitable job satisfying a baby's tummy, ensuring he'll have a good night's sleep and won't be awakened by hunger pangs. While you baby grows, his protein quota at lunchtime will be increasing. The recipes in this chapter are packed with veggies, but to keep your baby's protein intake up, you can serve them alongside some meat or fish.

Small bites
It's also at this age that your little gourmet is introduced to chunky food. No more smooth purées; you'll gradually introduce ones with roughly chopped pieces that can be mashed. His meals are starting to look more and more like your own!

Just like grown-ups
Now that he is sitting up straight and having fun gnawing on his crust of bread, why not invite him to the family dinner table? By integrating Baby naturally into your dinners, you're teaching him to see a meal as a moment to relax and share, a pleasurable time when he can interact with the family and taste the grown-up dishes, as long as they don't pose any danger (allergies or intolerances).

Ambience is everything

If your little one gets into the habit of eating dinner in a hurry, with the television going full blast and the family getting all worked up as dinnertime approaches, it's guaranteed his appetite or enthusiasm will reflect that. The pleasure of eating comes not only from the food itself, but from the atmosphere in which it is consumed.

A bit of advice

If you can't be there for Baby's dinner – on a regular or an occasional basis – avoid making a big entrance if you happen to arrive home during his mealtime. He's missed you so much during the long day that his attention will inevitably be focused on you. This is enough to make him push aside even the tastiest dishes in the world! So let him eat peacefully and say hello once he's had his dinner. Then you'll have plenty of time to hold and pamper him knowing that he's been well fed. Finally, make sure you don't tuck your baby into bed immediately after he's eaten. Would you like to go to bed after a good dish of risotto? Too heavy! Spend about an hour interacting and cuddling with him, preparing him for bedtime.

recipes with infinite (or almost infinite) combinations ...

Nothing's better than diversity for expanding Bébé's palate. For this reason I've separated the main dishes from their accompaniments (listed under *avec ...*) so you can vary the recipes on a whim. Try them with my suggestions or try out your own recipe combinations. Bébé will discover, to his delight, that he can enjoy Risotto Milanese *avec* Crushed Tomatoes *ou* Creamy Spinach. You can choose what to serve when, according to the season, the mood of the chef or the suggestions of your *petit gourmet*!

risotto Milanese
risotto Milanais

| 5 | 20 | 24ʰ | -18˚ |

Makes five 100g (3½oz) servings

1 tablespoon olive oil
2 teaspoons finely chopped shallots
150g (5½oz) Arborio rice
4 tablespoons low-salt vegetable stock
500ml (17fl oz) water
100g (3½oz) Parmesan, grated
1 tablespoon crème fraîche

1. In a heavy-based saucepan, heat the olive oil over a medium heat and brown the shallots.
2. Add the rice. Stir and cook for several minutes until the rice is mostly translucent.
3. Add the vegetable stock and half of the water and bring to the boil. Lower the heat and cook for 7 minutes, stirring regularly.
4. Gradually add the rest of the water and continue cooking, stirring regularly for about 10 minutes, until the rice is tender.
5. Remove from the heat, add the Parmesan and the crème fraîche and stir. The risotto should be smooth and creamy. If it is dry, add a few tablespoons of hot water and stir until you reach the desired consistency.

yummy tips

To entertain Bébé, remove the insides of a beef tomato and serve the risotto inside it. Guaranteed success! This is how Maya learnt to appreciate fresh tomatoes, as she loved eating her 'bowl'!

This risotto is just as good for grown-ups as it is for kids. When I eat with my children, I simply add a pinch of salt and serve it alongside a roast chicken breast with lemon.

avec ... crushed tomatoes and carrots

concassé de tomates et carottes

Makes five 100g (3½oz) servings

400g (14oz) tomatoes
250g (9oz) carrots
1 teaspoon olive oil
½ garlic clove, finely chopped
4–5 basil leaves

1. Wash the vegetables. Cut the tomatoes into quarters. Peel the carrots and cut them into thin rounds.
2. In a heavy-based saucepan, heat the olive oil over a medium heat and brown the garlic. Add the vegetables, lower the heat, cover and simmer for 10–12 minutes. Do not add water; the tomatoes should provide enough liquid so long as the heat is kept low. Add the basil leaves and cook for a further 3 minutes.
3. Remove from the heat and blend the mixture until you have a texture that's somewhere between chopped and mashed, depending on Bébé's preference.

yummy tips

Though I prefer to serve the risotto and the crushed tomatoes and carrots side by side (to better appreciate their flavours), they also happen to taste great combined.

avec ... butternut squash with sage

potimarron et à la sauge

⏰	🍲	▭	❄
10	15	24ʰ	-18°

Makes five 100g (3½oz) servings

500g (1lb 2oz) butternut squash
2 teaspoons olive oil
3–4 fresh sage leaves, finely chopped

1. Preheat the oven to 200°C (400°F/Gas Mark 6).
2. Remove the squash skin and seeds and dice the flesh into small cubes.
3. Spread the squash cubes on a baking tray covered with foil and coat the cubes with the olive oil.
4. Bake in the centre of the oven for 15 minutes until the squash is tender and begins to brown.
5. Remove the baking tray from the oven and add the sage. Lightly crush the squash pieces with a fork before serving.

yummy tips

Can't find butternut squash? If you're looking for an alternative, carrots are better than pumpkin, as the latter contains too much water for this recipe. When using carrots, cut them into small cubes and boil them in water for 15 minutes instead of baking. When Maya was a bit older, she loved this mixed with Risotto Milanese (page 80) using half carrots, half sweetcorn and lots of sage.

fine semolina with orange

semoule fine à l'orange

⏱	🍲	🗄	❄
1	5	24ʰ	-18°

Makes one 100g
(3½oz) serving

5 tablespoons orange juice
50g (1¾oz) fine semolina

1. In a saucepan, bring the orange juice to the boil.
2. Remove the saucepan from heat, add the semolina and stir. Cover and leave the semolina to expand for 5 minutes.
3. Fluff the semolina with a fork before serving.

yummy tips

Is the semolina too dry on its own? If so, after the semolina expands mix in more orange juice (up to 100ml/3½fl oz) and 2 heaped tablespoons of Carrot Purée (page 36) to moisten it. If you serve it this way, you can easily prepare several servings in advance and freeze them.

avec ... vegetable tagine
un tajine de légumes

⏲	🍲	🗄	❄
10	20	24ʰ	-18°

Makes five 100g (3½oz) servings

115g (4oz) courgettes
100g (3½oz) carrots
200g (7oz) tomatoes
55g (2oz) aubergine
4 ready-to-eat dried apricots
2 teaspoons olive oil
½ garlic clove, chopped
Pinch of ground ginger
Pinch of ground cumin
Pinch of finely chopped fresh coriander
1 tablespoon tomato purée
100ml (3½fl oz) water

1. Wash the vegetables. Peel the carrots and cut all the vegetables into cubes. Chop the dried apricots.
2. In a heavy-based saucepan, heat the olive oil over a medium heat and brown the garlic. Add the spices, coriander and the apricots. Cook for 1 minute, stirring regularly. Add the vegetables, tomato purée and water. Bring to the boil. Lower the heat, cover and simmer over a low heat for 15 minutes.
3. Remove the saucepan from heat and blend the mixture until smooth.

yummy tips
You can start small and increase the quantity of spices in this recipe bit by bit until Bébé gets used to them. The first time you make this tagine, replace the ginger with 2 −3 drops of lemon juice and add just a touch of cumin.

avec ... ratatouille

une ratatouille

Makes five 100g (3½oz) servings

175g (6oz) courgettes
250g (9oz) tomatoes
250g (9oz) aubergine
2 teaspoons olive oil
½ garlic clove, chopped
2 teaspoons finely chopped shallots
1 tablespoon tomato purée
Pinch of dried thyme
100ml (3½fl oz) water

1. Wash the vegetables and cut them into medium-sized cubes.
2. In a heavy-based saucepan, heat the olive oil over a medium heat and sauté the garlic and shallots until golden. Add the vegetables, tomato purée and thyme. Add the water and bring to the boil. Cover and simmer over a low heat for 15 minutes.
3. Remove from heat and blend to obtain a rough texture.

yummy tips

For a luxurious take on this recipe, use cherry tomatoes instead of large ones. Add them whole so they release their juices slowly and don't over-cook. If you freeze one portion of this recipe, you'll be one step ahead when you want to make Tuna Niçoise with Thyme Semolina (page 110).

pasta shapes with soft cheese and basil
petites pâtes au fromage à tartiner et au basilic

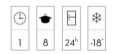

1   8   24ʰ   -18°

Makes one 100g
(3½oz) serving

*100g (3½oz) small pasta shapes (such
as mini-macaroni or alphabet shapes)
1 wedge or rounded teaspoon soft cheese,
such as Laughing Cow
4–5 fresh basil leaves, finely chopped*

1. Cook the pasta according to the packet instructions, with a pinch of salt.
2. Drain and return to the pan.
3. Add the cheese and basil and stir. Remove from the heat as soon as the cheese has melted.

yummy tips
As children get older, choose wholewheat or spelt pasta, both of which have a high nutritional value and a pleasant nutty taste. Richer in fibre than traditional pasta, they also aid in digestion.

ROSSO

avec ... primavera sauce
une sauce primavera

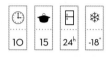

10 | 15 | 24ʰ | -18˚

Makes five 100g (3½oz) servings

115g (4oz) courgettes
100g (3½oz) broccoli florets
100g (3½oz) green beans
2 teaspoons olive oil
2 teaspoons finely chopped shallots
100g (3½oz) peas,
fresh or frozen
125ml (4fl oz) low-salt vegetable stock
3 tablespoons crème fraîche

1. Wash the courgettes and broccoli and cut them into small pieces. Trim the ends of the green beans and cut them into quarters.
2. In a heavy-based saucepan, heat the olive oil over a medium heat and cook the shallots until golden. Add the courgettes, broccoli, green beans, peas, vegetable stock and if necessary enough water to cover the vegetables halfway. Bring to the boil, then lower the heat, cover and cook for 10 minutes.
3. Drain the vegetables, setting aside about 3 tablespoons of the cooking liquid. Return the vegetables to the pan, add the crème fraîche and reheat the mixture with some of the reserved liquid.
4. Blend to a rough purée. Adjust the texture with the reserved cooking liquid if necessary.

yummy tips

You can speed up this recipe by using frozen vegetables, as they are pre-cut and washed. If you decide to serve this sauce over Pasta Shapes with Soft Cheese and Basil (page 88), opt for light crème fraîche so the sauce doesn't turn out too rich.

avec ... fresh tomato sauce

une sauce aux tomates fraîches

⏱	🥘	🗄	❄
5	20	24ʰ	-18˚

Makes five 100g (3½oz) servings

600g (1lb 5oz) tomatoes
2 teaspoons olive oil
½ garlic clove, finely chopped

1. Wash the tomatoes and cut them into quarters.
2. In a heavy-based saucepan, heat the olive oil over a medium-high heat and cook the garlic until golden.
3. Add the tomatoes, reduce the heat, cover and cook over a medium heat for 15–20 minutes (depending on the size of the tomatoes).
4. Remove from the heat and blend to a rough purée.

yummy tips

I like to make this recipe with cherry tomatoes, which are slightly sweeter than their larger counterparts. (It may be decadent, but hey, we'll tell Dr Lalau Keraly not to read this tip!) If you find the tomatoes too acidic, add 1 tablespoon of tomato ketchup to the sauce.

avec ... creamy spinach

épinards à la crème

5 | 12 | 24ʰ | -18°

Makes five 100g (3½oz) servings

500g (1lb 2oz) frozen spinach
125ml (4fl oz) low-salt vegetable stock
2 tablespoons crème fraîche

1. Put the frozen spinach into a saucepan. Add the vegetable stock and if necessary enough water to cover. Cover and bring to the boil.
2. Reduce the heat to medium and cook for 10 minutes.
3. Drain thoroughly; spinach retains plenty of water. Add the crème fraîche and return to the saucepan to heat through.
4. Blend until you have a rough purée.

yummy tips

Served with pasta, this recipe may at first seem like an unusual combination. But trust me, it's simply delicious. The slightly acidic notes in both the spinach and the crème fraîche are marvellous with all kinds of pasta. When I eat with the kids, I roast a salmon fillet in the oven to go along with this dish.

avec ... broad beans, ricotta and basil

fèves à la ricotta et au basilic

Makes five 100g (3½oz) servings

55g (2oz) courgette
400g (14oz) broad beans, frozen
125ml (4fl oz) low-salt vegetable stock
2 tablespoons ricotta
4–5 fresh basil leaves, finely chopped

1. Wash the courgette and cut it into small pieces.
2. Put the broad beans into a saucepan, add the vegetable stock and enough water to cover. Cover and bring to the boil. Lower the heat to medium and cook for 10 minutes. Add the courgette and cook for a further 5 minutes.
3. Drain, leaving about 3 tablespoons of cooking liquid in the pan.
4. Mix the vegetables with the remaining liquid, the ricotta and the basil.

yummy tips

If you can't find ricotta, use fresh goat's cheese. This recipe pairs well with Pasta Shapes with Soft Cheese and Basil (page 88), but then you should omit the soft cheese.

braised green lentils and spinach
étuvée de lentilles vertes et épinards

⏰	🍲	🗄	❄
5	30	24ʰ	-18°

Makes five 150g (5oz) servings

200g (7oz) green or Puy lentils
300g (10½oz) frozen spinach
125ml (4fl oz) low-salt vegetable stock

1. Rinse the lentils, picking over them and discarding any stones or debris.
2. Put the lentils into a saucepan and cover them with twice their volume of water. Bring to the boil, reduce the heat, cover and cook over a medium heat for 30 minutes or until the lentils are tender.
3. While the lentils are cooking, cook the spinach in the vegetable stock in another saucepan over a medium heat for 10 minutes.
4. Remove the spinach from the heat, drain and give it a quick stir.
5. Drain the lentils and mix in the spinach.

accompaniments
Serve with basmati rice or bread topped with fresh soft cheese.

yummy tips
When the grown-ups sit down to dinner with the kids, I serve this dish along with a roasted cod fillet enhanced with a few drops of fresh lemon juice.

pumpkin, sweet potato and vanilla soup
velouté de potiron et de patates douces à la vanille

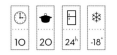

Makes five 200g (7oz) servings

*300g (10½oz) pumpkin
or butternut squash
450g (1lb) sweet potatoes
250ml (9fl oz) low-salt vegetable stock
700ml (1¼ pints) water
1 vanilla pod
2 tablespoons crème fraîche
2 teaspoons lemon juice*

1. Peel and deseed the pumpkin or squash and cut the flesh into pieces.
2. Wash and peel the sweet potatoes and cut them into cubes.
3. Put the vegetables into a large saucepan. Add the vegetable stock and the water. With a knife, open the vanilla pod lengthways and scrape the seeds into the pan. Add the pod to the pan.
4. Bring the mixture to the boil. Cover and cook over a medium heat for 20 minutes.
5. Remove from the heat and discard the vanilla pod.
6. Add the crème fraîche and lemon juice and blend until smooth.
7. The soup should be creamy. If it is too thick, simply add some water. If it is too wet, boil some additional sweet potato or potato, add to the mixture and blend again.

yummy tips

The flavours in this soup offer an excellent opportunity to introduce Bébé to mushrooms. When Maya was little, I used to chop some mushrooms and sauté them in a bit of butter before placing them on top of the soup. She loved them! Nowadays, she happily chomps on raw mushrooms.

broccoli and cheese soup
soupe aux brocolis et au fromage à tartiner

Makes five 200g (7oz) servings

400g (14oz) broccoli florets
1 teaspoon olive oil
2 teaspoons finely chopped shallots
250ml (9fl oz) low-salt vegetable stock
700ml (1¼ pints) water
4 wedges or rounded teaspoons soft
cheese, such as Laughing Cow

1. Wash the broccoli and cut into small pieces.
2. In a heavy-based saucepan, heat the olive oil over a medium-high heat and cook the shallots for 1 minute or until translucent. Add the vegetable stock, water and broccoli and bring to the boil. Reduce the heat, cover and cook for 10 minutes.
3. Remove from the heat, add the soft cheese and blend until smooth.
4. The soup should be creamy. If it is too thick, add a little water. If it is too wet, boil some broccoli florets, add them to the soup and blend again.

accompaniments
Serve with a bit of fresh bread, if Bébé likes it.

yummy tips
For babies over twelve months, liven up this soup with a bit of ground nutmeg. You can also try leaving a few whole broccoli florets in the middle of the soup, to give those new teeth something to bite on!

cream of sweetcorn and tomatoes
crème de maïs et tomates

🕐	🍲	🗄	❄
5	15	24ʰ	-18˚

Makes five 200g (7oz) servings

250g (9oz) tomatoes
300g (10½oz) sweetcorn,
frozen or tinned
4 fresh sage leaves, chopped
250ml (9fl oz) low-salt vegetable stock
700ml (1¼ pints) water
2 tablespoons crème fraîche

1. Wash the tomatoes and cut them into quarters.
2. Put the sweetcorn, tomatoes and sage into a big saucepan, add the vegetable stock and water and bring to the boil. Cover and cook over a medium heat for 15 minutes.
3. Remove from the heat, add the crème fraîche and blend until smooth.
4. The soup should be creamy. If it is too thick, add a little water. If it is too wet, add some sweetcorn directly to the mixture, cook for an additional 5–7 minutes and blend again.

yummy tips
Your 'big baby' will probably be delighted to crunch on a few whole sweetcorn kernels, so leave a few in the soup!

Chiara, 20 months, official taster

first big kid lunches

&

big kid dinners with the family

12 months+

BIG KID LUNCHES, BIG KID DINNERS

Dr Jean Lalau Keraly, paediatric nutritionist and endocrinologist

One year old already! Your little one has sprouted up at the speed of light, thanks largely to the good meals you've lovingly prepared for her. After some occasionally laborious weeks of gradually introducing new foods, her twelve-month-old body is able to digest big kid food. The list of forbidden foods is dwindling and all foods now are allowed, apart from whole nuts (except for those who have been diagnosed with allergies). Your baby can now sit at the family table and share meals with her parents and brothers or sisters, with textures adapted to her needs.

Baby teeth

At twelve months, not all babies are in fact equal; those cutting their baby teeth are able to consume increasingly bigger chunks. Others boast a wide, toothless smile and are still in the minced or mashed phase. Don't panic: each baby has her own rhythm. As the first baby teeth appear, the transition to 'biting' her food will take place naturally. It's up to you to adapt and progressively guide your little one to appreciate meals that have more texture.

Slightly bigger bites

Limiting your baby to exclusively minced or mashed foods is truly depriving her of the richness of flavours that bits of meat, vegetables and fruits can add to her diet. Doing so keeps her in a 'baby' stage, which will eventually damage her development of motor skills and her rapport with a normal diet. No need to hurry, which will only frighten and upset her. Simply keep in mind that when your child is older than eighteen months, it's recommended to proceed to dishes with substantial chunks.

Holding her own baby spoon

This is around the time that Baby will gradually free herself from her parents' assistance with feeding. It's not easy using a spoon on her own. But what fun it is for her to pick up chunks of tender courgette and put them into her own mouth! Experiencing this kind of freedom is what's important at your toddler's developmental stage. The more independent she becomes, the better your chances to march her down the path to healthy eating. Not only is she acquiring an autonomy that will be useful in her general development, she's also taking charge of her own diet. She's becoming an actor, not just a spectator. Baby is growing up!

But be careful!

Though Baby's diet will resemble the rest of the family's from now on, it doesn't mean you should let her pick up the family's bad eating habits. After months of paying scrupulous attention to expanding their baby's food horizons, parents tend to lose steam by the time their little one has blown out her first birthday candles and they gradually invest less time in preparing her meals. So baby meals tend to become an exact copy of the family's, which means they become more simplified and less varied – with fewer fruits and vegetables and too much salt and meat.

A balanced diet

Obviously, you will not make this error. If Baby can now eat as you do, it's the right time to pass on the good habits you've established during your little one's initiation to taste – but this time you should also pass them on to the rest of the family. In summary, good habits include lots of vegetables, fruits, a mix of white and wholegrain cereals, dairy foods or calcium-rich alternatives, a little protein, fewer bad fats and fewer sugars. It doesn't mean you're going to put the whole family on a diet! Throughout this book, you've noticed that eating well doesn't go hand in hand with eating low-fat, bland foods. So offer your baby well-balanced recipes without too much protein (up to age two, no more than 40g /1½oz of meat or fish daily) and an important supply of iron and calcium. Also don't forget that your big kid, at this age, no longer always needs a snack between meals, if they are only a few hours apart, or a bottle of milk during the night.

In this chapter

In this chapter dedicated to our big kids, you'll find savoury and sweet recipes that take into account recommendations from healthcare officials and the pressures of modern parenting, along with the desires of your budding gastronome, who is starting to know and identify her favourite dishes. You're not about to complain, as it was you who launched the taste initiation in the first place. It is finally time for her to take the lead gently, vis-à-vis her culinary preferences. It's by considering food a source of pleasure and discovery and not of stress or obligation that your baby will continue to navigate along the path of (good) taste.

something's cooking!

Introducing Bébé to gastronomy is not about being tied down to the home-cooked dishes we loved as children – our elbows on the dinner table, impatiently waiting for Granny's steaming ladle to fill our desperately empty bowl. Keeping in mind that our grandmothers' tried-and-true recipes were not always completely focused on the nutritional needs of our littlest ones, I made adjustments to them, taking inspiration from the best aspects of the previous generation's incomparable cuisine. So in these pages you'll find one-pot meals specifically designed for kids ages one and over and bursting with vitamins and flavour. And, just between us, if you want to double or triple the recipe for the whole family's enjoyment, that's allowed too.

chicken and vegetables in coconut milk
poulet au lait de coco et petits legumes

15	20	24ʰ	-18°

Makes five 120g
(4¼oz) servings

100g (3½oz) carrots
55g (2oz) courgette
100g (3½oz) green beans
5–6 broccoli florets
1 chicken breast, about 100g (3½oz)
1 tablespoon sunflower oil
1 garlic clove, finely chopped
½ teaspoon ground ginger
200ml (7fl oz) coconut milk
1 tablespoon lemon juice
Pinch each of salt and soft brown sugar
100ml (3½fl oz) water
3–4 fresh coriander leaves, chopped

1. Wash the vegetables and peel the carrots. Cut the courgette and carrots into rounds. Trim the green beans and cut them into pieces. Roughly chop the broccoli florets. Cut the chicken breast into pieces.
2. Heat the sunflower oil over a medium heat in a large, heavy-based saucepan and cook the chicken pieces until golden brown.
3. Add the garlic and ginger and continue cooking for 1 minute, without browning too much.
4. Add the vegetables, coconut milk, lemon juice, salt, brown sugar and water and bring to the boil. Cover and simmer over a low heat for 15 minutes.
5. Remove from the heat, add the coriander and blend until you have a coarse purée.

accompaniments
Serve with basmati rice. For one portion, boil 100ml (3½fl oz) water in a saucepan. Add 50g (1¾oz) rice, cover and cook over a low heat for 15 minutes or until the water is completely absorbed.

yummy tips
Is Bébé not wild about coconut milk? Replace it with crème fraîche and leave out the lemon juice. The crème fraîche already has the slightly acidic note this dish calls for.

chicken tagine with sultanas
tajine de poulet aux raisins secs

10	30	24ʰ	-18°

Makes five 120g
(4¹/₄oz) servings

325g (1½ lb) carrots
55g (2oz) courgette
200g (7oz) tomatoes
1 tablespoon olive oil
1 chicken thigh, about 225g (8oz)
1 onion, finely chopped
1 garlic clove, finely chopped
Pinch of salt
½ teaspoon ground ginger
½ teaspoon ground mixed spice
1 tablespoon sultanas
200ml (7fl oz) orange juice
100ml (3½fl oz) water

1. Wash the vegetables and peel the carrots. Cut the carrots and the courgette into rounds and cut the tomatoes into quarters.
2. Heat the olive oil in a large, heavy-based saucepan over a medium heat and brown the chicken thigh (skin-side down). Add the onion, garlic, salt and spices and continue cooking for a further minute, without browning too much.
3. Add the vegetables, half the sultanas, the orange juice and water. Cover and let simmer over a low heat for 15 minutes. Add the other half of the sultanas and cook for a further 10 minutes.
4. Remove from the heat and take out the chicken thigh. Remove the bones and skin. Put the meat back into the mixture and blend roughly until you have a rough purée.

accompaniments
Serve this tagine with Fine Semolina with Thyme (page 69).

yummy tips

For bigger kids, prepare this dish through step 3 with chicken drumsticks. Perfect for eating with their fingers!

lamb tagine with apricots
tajine d'agneau aux abricots secs

Makes five 120g (4¼oz) servings

250g (9oz) carrots
125g (4oz) courgettes
200g (7oz) tomatoes
100g (3½oz) leg of lamb
(or shoulder)
1 tablespoon olive oil
1 garlic clove, finely chopped
Pinch of salt
½ teaspoon ground ginger
½ teaspoon ground mixed spice
10 ready-to-eat dried apricots

1. Wash the vegetables and peel the carrots. Cut the carrots and courgettes into rounds and cut the tomatoes into quarters. Trim the fat from the lamb and cut it into pieces.

2. Heat the olive oil in a large, heavy-based saucepan over a medium heat and brown the lamb pieces on all sides. Add the garlic, salt and spices and cook for a further minute, without browning too much.

3. Add the vegetables and half the dried apricots and cover them halfway with water. Bring to the boil, cover and simmer over a low heat for 15 minutes. Add the rest of the apricots and continue cooking for a further 10 minutes.

4. Remove from the heat and blend roughly until you have a rough purée.

accompaniments
Serve this tagine with Fine Semolina with Thyme (page 69) or Fine Semolina with Orange (page 84).

yummy tips
For grown-ups, this tagine needs more zing! Liven it up with a dash of Tabasco sauce or cayenne pepper. For crunchiness, add a handful of blanched almonds to the mixture just after cooking. Sprinkle a bit of cinnamon over the semolina.

Italian meatballs
boulettes de viande comme en Italie

| 20 | 25 | 24ʰ | -18˚ |

Makes five 120g (4¼oz) servings

For the meatballs
100g (3½oz) minced beef
½ onion, finely chopped
1 potato, cooked and mashed
Pinch of salt
Freshly ground pepper to taste

For the tomato sauce
200g (7oz) tomatoes
2 teaspoons olive oil
1 teaspoon finely chopped garlic
1 tablespoon tomato purée
4 fresh basil leaves, chopped

1. Mix together the minced beef, onion, mashed potato, salt, and pepper. Make small balls (about 15) and leave to sit for 10–15 minutes at room temperature.
2. Wash the tomatoes and cut them into quarters.
3. In a heavy-based saucepan, heat half of the olive oil over a medium heat and cook the garlic until lightly golden but not brown. Add the tomatoes, tomato purée and basil. Cover and simmer for 10 minutes.
4. Heat the rest of the olive oil in another pan over a medium heat and carefully add the meatballs. Brown them on all sides so that they are sealed, meaning you can no longer see any raw meat on the outside.
5. Remove the tomato sauce from the heat and blend. Add the meatballs and cook over a low heat for about 10 minutes or until the meatballs are cooked through.

accompaniments
Serve these meatballs with cooked pasta shapes sprinkled with a bit of grated Parmesan.

yummy tips
Sometimes I find it too laborious and time-consuming to make my own meatballs, so I often use frozen mini-meatballs. Heating them up in the tomato sauce takes 10 minutes and couldn't be easier!

baby beef bourguignon
boeuf bourguignon spécial bébé

Makes five 120g
(4¼oz) servings

250g (9oz) carrots
115g (4oz) courgettes
200g (7oz) tomatoes

100g (3½oz) stewing steak
2 teaspoons olive oil
½ onion, finely chopped
2 rashers of bacon or 2 slices cooked ham
1 tablespoon tomato purée
½ teaspoon dried thyme
Freshly ground pepper to taste
1 bay leaf

1. Wash vegetables and peel the carrots. Cut the carrots and courgettes into rounds and cut the tomatoes into quarters. Cut the steak into pieces.
2. In a heavy-based saucepan, heat the olive oil over a medium heat. Brown the steak pieces on all sides. Add the onions and bacon and continue to cook for 1 minute without browning too much.
3. Add the vegetables, tomato purée, thyme, pepper and bay leaf and cover halfway with water. Bring to the boil, cover and simmer over a low heat for 25 minutes.
4. Remove from the heat, take out the bay leaf and blend until you have a rough purée.

accompaniments
This bourguignon is well paired with Old-Fashioned Mashed Potatoes (page 68).

yummy tips
I top this dish off with caramelised chestnuts. They're Maya's favourite — and super-easy to prepare! Buy vacuum-packed chestnuts. In a frying pan, melt a knob of butter over a low heat and gently sauté the chestnuts with a generous pinch of soft brown sugar (or white sugar if that's all you have). Turn the chestnuts constantly, until the sugar melts and the chestnuts are good and hot.

express lunches for busy days

In our hectic lives as overactive parents, we can't always spend half an hour in front of the hob simmering, braising, chopping and elaborating inventive recipes. Between the shopping (not to mention unloading and putting away the groceries), the picking up at school and the getting to the doctor's on time, your schedule is starting to make the Prime Minister's look like a Boy Scout leader's! With this shortage of time in mind, I created a handful of 'express recipes' – ready in the blink of an eye but still just as appetising and nutrition-rich as the others in this book. Who's getting a gold star?

tuna Niçoise with thyme semolina
thon à la Niçoise et semoule fine au thym

⏱	●	⊞	❄
2	5	24ʰ	-18°

Makes one 120g (4¼oz) serving

*100g (3½oz) ratatouille
(which you wisely froze the last time
you made it – see page 87)
30g (1oz) tinned tuna in water
4 tablespoons water
½ teaspoon dried thyme
Pinch of salt
50g (1¾oz) fine semolina*

1. Heat the ratatouille in a saucepan over a medium heat.
2. Drain the tuna and fluff it with a fork.
3. Mix the tuna into the ratatouille, reduce the heat and cook for 5 minutes.
4. Meanwhile, bring the water to the boil. Add the thyme, salt and semolina. Cover and leave to sit for 5 minutes (giving the semolina time to expand).
5. Fluff the semolina with a fork and serve with the tuna Niçoise.

yummy tips

This dish can also be made with Fresh Tomato Sauce (page 91), which you have (of course) prepared in advance and can therefore pop out of your freezer whenever you need it!

pasta with ham and peas

pâtes au jambon blanc et petits pois

2	5	24ʰ	-18°

Makes one 120g
(4¼oz) serving

100g (3½oz) pasta shapes
50g (1¾oz) peas, fresh or frozen
10g (¼oz) butter
1 teaspoon finely chopped shallots
1 slice ham, cut into bite-sized pieces
2 tablespoons crème fraîche

1. Cook the pasta according to the packet instructions.
2. Meanwhile, bring a small saucepan of water to the boil, add the peas and cook for 5 minutes. Drain and put them back into the pan.
3. Return the pan to the heat and add the butter, shallots and ham. Cook for 1–2 minutes, stirring constantly.
4. Add the crème fraîche and bring to the boil, then remove from the heat.
5. Drain the pasta. Serve topped with the ham and pea sauce.

yummy tips

To speed up recipes like this one, I always keep a supply of finely chopped shallots, garlic and onions in my freezer. If you have them handy, you won't even need a chopping board to make this simple pasta dish.

chicken with broccoli and basmati rice

poulet aux brocolis et riz basmati

5 10

Makes one 120g (4¼oz) serving

250ml (9fl oz) water
50g (1¾oz) basmati rice
1 teaspoon olive oil
1 teaspoon finely chopped shallots
30g (1oz) chicken breast,
cut into small pieces
50g (1¾oz) broccoli florets
2 tablespoons crème fraîche
1 tablespoon grated Parmesan

1. Bring half of the water to the boil in a saucepan with the rice and a pinch of salt. Reduce the heat, cover and cook for 10 minutes or until the water is completely absorbed.
2. In a heavy-based saucepan, heat the olive oil, add the shallots and cook for 1 minute.
3. Add the chicken pieces and brown them on all sides. Add the remaining water and the broccoli florets. Cook, uncovered, for a further 7 minutes.
4. Add the crème fraîche and the Parmesan. Simmer for 2–3 minutes. Serve with the rice.

yummy tips

This dish can be made with all kinds of white meat: chicken, turkey, veal and even pork. Use whatever you have. I don't recommend using a lighter cheese than Parmesan — the chicken and broccoli benefit from its saltiness.

now I can eat like everyone else

It's here! The moment all parent chefs eagerly await: when Bébé can eat like the rest of the family. At one year he's ready to take that step. You can finally stop dividing your brain into two – or even three – parts in order to juggle the daily menus for Bébé, Little Brother, Big Sister and the grown-ups. In these pages you'll find recipes suited for little and big palates! The difference that remains, above all, is what is done to the food after it's prepared. You'll serve the dish as is to the older family members and adjust the preparation (that is, its texture) to fit Bébé's needs: slices if he likes eating those or roughly blended if he prefers smoother meals. But with these recipes, sharing is the name of the game. Everyone can enjoy themselves around the table with the same yummy dish. For Bébé taking full part in this ritual is a precious moment in his gustatory learning process. Enjoy the family meal!

turkey escalope with Parma ham, sweet potato purée and peas

escalope de dinde au jambon de Parme, purée de patates douces et petits pois

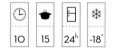

🕐	🍲	🗄	❄
10	15	24ʰ	-18˚

Makes 2 adult portions and 1 baby portion

450g (1lb) sweet potatoes
2 turkey escalopes,
about 150g (5oz) each
2½ slices Parma ham
200g (7oz) peas, fresh or frozen
10g (¼oz) butter

1. Wash and peel the sweet potatoes. Cut them into cubes.
2. Put the sweet potato cubes into a saucepan and cover with water. Bring to the boil, lower the heat and simmer for 15 minutes.
3. Preheat the oven to 200°C (400°F/Gas Mark 6).
4. Cut a thin slice off one of the escalopes for Bébé. Roll the escalopes inside a slice of ham each. Then roll the slice of escalope inside the ½ slice of ham.
5. Put the turkey escalopes on to a baking tray covered with foil. Bake the grown-ups' escalopes for 10–12 minutes. Halfway through the baking time, add Bébé's mini-escalope to the oven.
6. Halfway through the baking time, put the peas into a saucepan, cover with water and bring to the boil. Cook them over a medium heat for 5 minutes.
7. Meanwhile, drain the sweet potatoes. Mash the potatoes and butter with a fork until you have a smooth purée.
8. Remove the turkey escalopes from the oven. Roughly chop Bébé's piece. Serve with the sweet potato purée and the peas (blended for Bébé if necessary).

yummy tips

Roast the sweet potatoes in the oven to enhance their flavour. Cook the sweet potato cubes on the baking tray with the turkey escalopes. To serve, mash them for Bébé – and add a splash of olive oil and a sprinkle of sea salt for the grown-ups.

cod papillote with orange
papillote de cabillaud à l'orange

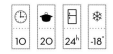

10	20	24ʰ	-18˚

Makes 2 adult portions
and 1 baby portion

*2 full-sized cod fillets, about 200g (7oz)
each and 1 small fillet,
about 20g (¾oz) for Bébé
10 cherry tomatoes
1 orange
5 fresh coriander leaves, finely chopped
500g (1lb 2oz) broccoli florets*

1. Preheat the oven to 180°C (350°F/Gas Mark 4).
2. Place each cod fillet on a large square of foil twice its size. Make sure Bébé's piece has no bones.
3. Wash the cherry tomatoes and the orange and cut 5 round orange slices.
4. Place 2 orange slices and 4 cherry tomatoes on each grown-up's fillet and 1 orange slice and 2 cherry tomatoes on Bébé's small fillet. Squeeze the rest of the orange (discard any pips) and coat the fish with the juice. Add the coriander leaves to the papillotes before sealing them carefully. Bake the grown-ups' papillotes in the preheated oven for 20 minutes. Halfway through the cooking time, put Bébé's papillote into the oven.
5. Meanwhile, wash the broccoli florets. Put them into a pan with water and boil them for 10 minutes. Drain and blend them to a smooth purée.
6. Take the papillotes out of the oven. Serve the grown-up portions with the foil open. For Bébé's portion, remove the foil and serve the fish on a plate along with the broccoli purée.

yummy tips
If you want a more substantial meal, serve this dish alongside Old-Fashioned Mashed Potatoes (page 68).

oven-baked salmon with broad beans, lemon and basil

saumon au four avec fèves au citron et basilic

5	15	24ʰ	-18˚

Makes 2 adult portions and 1 baby portion

*2 full-sized salmon steaks, about 150g
(5oz) each and 1 small steak,
about 20g (¾oz), for Bébé
Pinch of salt
200g (7oz) broad beans, frozen
Juice from 1 lemon
6 fresh basil leaves, chopped*

1. Preheat the oven to 200°C (400°F/Gas Mark 6).
2. Place each of the grown-ups' salmon steaks on a baking tray covered with a piece of foil twice its size. Make sure Bébé's piece has no bones. Put it aside.
3. Sprinkle the grown-ups' steaks with a few grains of salt, then put them in the oven and cook for 15 minutes. Halfway through the cooking time, put the small steak for Bébé into the oven.
4. Halfway through the cooking time, bring a pan of water to the boil and add the broad beans. Cook over a medium heat for 7–10minutes. Remove from the heat and drain. Add the lemon juice and basil.
5. Take the salmon steaks out of the oven and leave to cool. Serve alongside the broad beans with lemon and basil. If wished, blend to a smooth purée for Bébé.

yummy tips

This dish goes well with Carrot Purée (page 36) blended with 15g (½oz) of butter and a pinch of salt.

two-fish pie with vegetables

parmentier de deux poissons et petits légumes

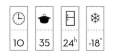

10	35	24ʰ	-18°

Makes 2 adult portions
and 1 baby portion

5 Anya potatoes
100g (3½oz) green beans
150g (5oz) peas, fresh or frozen
1 salmon fillet, about 200g (7oz)
1 cod fillet, about 150g (5oz)
100ml (3½fl oz) crème fraîche
2 teaspoons lemon juice
4 fresh basil leaves, chopped
10g (¼oz) butter
2 tablespoons full-fat milk
Pinch of salt
Pinch of ground nutmeg

1. Preheat the oven to 180°C (350°F/Gas Mark 4).
2. Wash and peel the potatoes and cut them into pieces. Put the pieces into a saucepan, cover them with water, bring to the boil and cook for 15 minutes.
3. Meanwhile, trim the green beans. Put the beans and peas into another pan, cover the vegetables with water, bring them to the boil and cook for 3–4 minutes. Drain and roughly chop the vegetables with a knife.
4. Cut the fish fillets into pieces. Make sure there are no bones.
5. Place the fish pieces at the base of a deep, ovenproof casserole. Cover with the drained green vegetables. Coat the fish and vegetables with the crème fraîche mixed with the lemon juice and basil.
6. Drain the potatoes and mash them with the butter, milk, salt and nutmeg. Cover the fish and vegetable mixture with the mashed potatoes and bake in the centre of the preheated oven for 20 minutes.
7. If Bébé is not yet used to eating chunks of food, mash the pieces of fish.

yummy tips

Infinite combinations are possible with this recipe. Replace the cod with another firm white fish, such as monkfish, and vary the vegetables. You might try broccoli or cauliflower, thin rounds of carrot or even fennel, if you dare.

I can eat by myself just like a big kid!

You're finally there – at the phase every parent will know sooner or later: boredom with familiar foods. It's no illness, simply a tough (and natural) period when your child starts to shrink from dishes she once loved. It's also the time Bébé wants to do everything alone 'like a big kid'. And eating tops her list. So I created these funny little galettes (think fancy fritters) that pack in – some would say *camouflage* – some serious quantities of vegetables, an ideal situation whenever your little gourmet makes a face at a plate of her former favourite broccoli. It's also a good way to let your little one gain some autonomy by crunching, dipping and rolling her evening galette all by herself. After that, vegetables will once again become her favourite dish. Want to bet?

carrot-courgette-lentil galettes
galettes de carottes-courgettes-lentilles

10   30   24ʰ   -18°

Makes 20 galettes
(five servings)

For the galettes
450g (1 lb) carrots
125ml (4fl oz) orange juice
½ teaspoon ground cumin
125ml (4fl oz) vegetable stock
300g (10½oz) red lentils
175g (6oz) courgettes
2 teaspoons olive oil

For the dipping sauce (1 serving)
125ml (4fl oz) natural,
unsweetened Greek yogurt
4 fresh coriander leaves, chopped

1. Wash and peel the carrots, then cut them into rounds.
2. Put the carrots orange juice, cumin and vegetable stock into a saucepan and add just enough water to cover. Bring to the boil and cook for 5 minutes.
3. Add the lentils and continue to cook for a further 10 minutes.
4. Meanwhile, wash the courgettes and grate them.
5. At the end of the cooking time, add the grated courgettes, drain and blend roughly.
6. Form the mixture into small galettes, about 3cm (1¼ inches) in diameter and 1cm (½ inch) thick. Leave them to sit for a few minutes on kitchen paper to absorb some of their moisture.
7. Heat 1 teaspoon of the olive oil in a large non-stick pan over a medium-high heat. Brown 10 galettes, cooking them 3–5 minutes on each side, then place them on kitchen paper and leave them to cool. Repeat.
8. Mix the yogurt with the coriander to make a dipping sauce.
9. Serve the galettes with a small bowl of the yogurt sauce.
Let Bébé eat the galettes with her fingers and dunk them into the sauce.

yummy tips

Why not make these galettes for yourself? For a light meal, serve the galettes with a grilled chicken breast dusted with cumin, paprika and curry powder and then sprinkled with olive oil and lemon juice. Add a pinch of cayenne pepper to the yogurt sauce and you have a flavourful dinner.

cheesy sweetcorn and carrot galettes
galettes de maïs-carottes-comté

⏰	🍲	🧊	❄
10	30	24ʰ	-18˚

Makes 20 galettes
(five servings)

For the galettes
400g (14oz) carrots
125ml (4fl oz) vegetable stock
200g (7oz) sweetcorn,
frozen or tinned
200g (7oz) Comté cheese, grated
½ teaspoon paprika
2 teaspoons olive oil

For the avocado purée
½ ripe avocado
3 drops lemon juice

1. Wash and peel the carrots, then cut them into rounds.
2. Put the carrots and vegetable stock into a saucepan and, if necessary, add water to cover. Bring to the boil, reduce the heat and cook for 10 minutes. Add the sweetcorn and cook for a further 5–7 minutes.
3. Drain the vegetables. Add the cheese and paprika and mix until the cheese starts to melt. Blend until you have a rough purée.
4. Form the mixture into small galettes, about 3cm (1¼ inches) in diameter and 1cm (½ inch) thick. Leave them to sit for a few minutes on kitchen paper to absorb some of their moisture.
5. Heat 1 teaspoon of the olive oil in a large, non-stick pan over a medium-high heat. Brown 10 galettes, cooking them 3–5 minutes on each side, then place them on kitchen paper and leave them to cool. Repeat.
6. Just before you are ready to serve the meal, cut open the avocado and remove the stone.
7. Scoop out the avocado flesh and put it into a bowl with the lemon juice (to preserve the green colour). Mash until you have a smooth purée.
8. Serve the galettes with the avocado purée. Let Bébé eat the galettes with his fingers and dunk them into the purée.

yummy tips
These galettes make a perfect starter for that special dinner with friends. If you would like them to be crisp, just leave them in the pan for an extra minute or two. Upgrade the avocado purée to a real guacamole by mixing 2 avocados with the juice of ½ lemon or lime, 2 tablespoons chopped onion, ½ teaspoon salt and a pinch each of cumin and cayenne. Dunk without moderation.

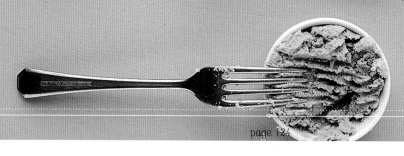

cheesy broccoli and broad bean galettes
galettes brocolis-fèves-parmesan

Makes 20 galettes
(five servings)

For the tomato sauce
600g (1lb 5oz) cherry tomatoes
1 teaspoon olive oil
½ garlic clove, finely chopped

For the galettes
400g (14oz) broccoli
400g (14oz) broad beans, frozen
125ml (4fl oz) vegetable stock
100g (3½oz) Parmesan, grated
4 fresh basil leaves
1 teaspoon olive oil

1. Start the sauce by washing the tomatoes and cutting them into halves.
2. In a heavy-based saucepan, heat 1 teaspoon of the olive oil and add the garlic. Brown the garlic, then add the tomatoes and lower the heat. Cover and cook over a medium heat for 15–20 minutes. Remove the pan from the heat and stir the tomatoes until you have a chunky sauce.
3. Meanwhile, for the galettes, wash the broccoli florets and cut them into small pieces.
4. Put the broccoli, broad beans and vegetable stock into a saucepan and add just enough water to cover. Bring to the boil, reduce the heat and cook for 10 minutes. Drain the vegetables.
5. Mix the drained vegetables, the Parmesan and basil until the cheese starts to melt. Blend until you have a smooth purée (it's important to blend well because the starch in the broad beans will hold the galettes together).
6. Form the mixture into small galettes, about 3cm (1¼ inches) in diameter and 1cm (½ inch) thick. Leave them to sit for a few minutes on kitchen paper to absorb some of their moisture.
7. Heat the remaining 1 teaspoon olive oil over a medium-high heat in a large non-stick pan. Brown 10 galettes, cooking them 3–5 minutes on each side, then place them on kitchen paper and let cool. Repeat for the remaining galettes.
8. Serve the galettes with the tomato sauce. Let Bébé eat the galettes with her fingers and dunk them into a cup of the sauce.

yummy tips
For a family lunch, serve these galettes with pan-fried chicken escalopes sprinkled with lemon juice and coated with tomato sauce.

'forgotten' vegetable galettes
galettes aux légumes oubliés

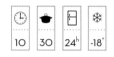

Makes 20 galettes
(five servings)

For the tomato-apple coulis
200g (7oz) tomatoes
350g (12oz) sweet apples
(Golden Delicious or similar)

For the galettes
200g (7oz) swede
55g (2oz) parsnip
100g (3½oz) celeriac
200g (7oz) potatoes
125ml (4fl oz) vegetable stock
2 teaspoons olive oil

1. Start the coulis by washing the tomatoes and apples. Peel the apples, remove the cores and any spare pips, then cut into cubes. Cut the tomatoes into quarters.
2. Put the tomatoes and apples into a saucepan and cover them with water. Bring to the boil, cover and simmer over a low heat for 15 minutes.
3. Meanwhile, for the galettes, wash the vegetables, then peel them and cut them into pieces.
4. Put the vegetables and stock into another pan and add just enough water to cover. Bring to the boil, lower the heat and cook for 15 minutes. Drain the vegetables. Blend until you have a chunky purée.
5. Form the mixture into small galettes, about 3cm (1¼ inches) in diameter and 1cm (½ inch) thick. Leave them to sit for a few minutes on kitchen paper to absorb some of their moisture.
6. Remove the tomatoes and apples from the heat and blend until you have a smooth coulis.
7. Heat 1 teaspoon of the olive oil in a large non-stick pan over a medium heat. Brown 10 galettes, cooking them 3–5 minutes on each side, then place them on kitchen paper and leave to cool. Repeat for the remaining galettes.
8. Serve the galettes with a small side dish of tomato-apple coulis. Let Bébé eat the galettes with his fingers and dunk them into the coulis.

yummy tips
These galettes pair really well with fish – a cod fillet or piece of monkfish – roasted in the oven with a splash of olive oil and a dash of sea salt, then topped with the tomato-apple coulis.

polenta chips with tomato and red pepper relish
bâtonnets de polenta avec tomates et poivrons rouges confits au four

⏰	🍲	🗄	❄
5	30	24ʰ	-18°

Makes 7 polenta chips
(one serving) and five
100g (3½oz) portions of
relish (see Yummy Tips)

**For the tomato and
red pepper relish**
*600g (1lb 5oz) tomatoes
or cherry tomatoes
300g (10½oz) red peppers
1 tablespoon olive oil*

For the polenta chips
*125ml (4fl oz) full-fat milk
50g (1¾oz) dried polenta
50g (1¾oz) Parmesan, grated*

1. Preheat the oven to 150°C (300°F/Gas Mark 2).
2. Start the relish by washing the tomatoes and peppers. Deseed the peppers and cut them into thin slices. Cut the tomatoes into quarters. Spread the vegetables on a baking tray covered with foil. Drizzle the vegetables with the olive oil. Roast in the centre of the oven for 30 minutes.
3. Remove the vegetables from the oven and leave to cool. Blend or roughly chop according to Bébé's tastes.
4. Meanwhile, bring the milk to the boil in a saucepan, stirring constantly. Remove from the heat and add the polenta and Parmesan, stirring vigorously until you have a thick, smooth purée. Pour the polenta on to a tray or plate to form a square 1cm (½ inch) thick. Leave to cool, then cut into chips.
5. Serve the polenta chips with the tomato and red pepper relish. Freeze the remaining vegetables in small plastic containers.

yummy tips

I always set aside a bit of the tomato and red pepper relish to use as a chutney for grown-ups. It makes a great after-dinner treat served with a hard cheese (such as aged Comté or Beaufort).
If apricots are in season, try adding a few to the vegetables you roast. This version pairs really well with white meat or even grilled salmon steaks.

oh, pasta – kids' all-time favourite

Let's not forget pasta, the object of everyone's affection! Were you thinking that this baby food cookery book, defender of healthy eating, would pass it by? Of course not! I'm going to let you in on a secret: pasta is chock-full of nutritious benefits and is part of a healthy diet. The thing is not to overdo it – and to know how to prepare it (you can't go wrong with a home-made tomato-basil sauce). On top of that, these quick meals are ideal for busy nights. Everyone wins!

mini-tortellini with ricotta and green vegetables
petits tortellinis, ricotta et légumes verts

5   10

Makes one 225g (8oz) serving

¼ courgette
40g (1½oz) peas, fresh or frozen
20g (¾oz) green beans,
cut into small pieces
1 teaspoon olive oil
1 teaspoon finely chopped shallots
1 teaspoon chopped fresh basil
2 tablespoons ricotta
100g (3½oz) mini-tortellini

1. Wash the courgette. Cut it into thin rounds, then cut the rounds into quarters.
2. In a heavy-based saucepan, boil some water and toss in the courgette, peas and green beans. Cook for 5–7 minutes, then drain and set aside.
3. In the same saucepan, heat the olive oil over a medium heat and add the shallots. Cook for 1 minute, then add the vegetables and continue to cook for a further 3 minutes.
4. Remove the saucepan from the heat, add the basil and ricotta, reheat and set aside.
5. Meanwhile, cook the tortellini according to the packet instructions.
6. Drain the tortellini, then mix it with the vegetable and ricotta mixture. Serve the dish lukewarm on Bébé's favourite plate.

yummy tips

Want to ring the changes? Turn it into a baked lasagna for four instead, using fresh lasagna sheets and four times the amount of vegetables and ricotta. Take a 1-litre (1¾-pint) ovenproof casserole dish and start with a layer of lasagna sheets followed by the vegetables and ricotta, alternating layers until the dish is full. Finish with a layer of lasagna sheets, cover with a mixture of ricotta and Parmesan and bake at 180°C (350°F/Gas Mark 4) for 25 minutes.

farfalle with broccoli and Parmesan
farfalles aux brocolis et au parmesan

5   10

Makes one 225g (8oz) serving

100g (3½oz) broccoli florets
1 tablespoon olive oil
1 teaspoon finely chopped shallot
2 tablespoons grated Parmesan
55g (2oz) farfalle

1. Wash the broccoli florets and cut them into small pieces. Bring a pan of water to the boil and add the broccoli. Cook for 5–7 minutes, then drain and set aside.

2. Heat the olive oil in the same pan over a medium heat and add the shallots. Cook for 1 minute, then stir in the broccoli florets and cook for a further 3 minutes. Remove from the heat, add the Parmesan, reheat and set aside.

3. Meanwhile, cook the farfalle according to the packet instructions.

4. Drain the pasta, then combine it with the broccoli and Parmesan mixture.

yummy tips

This simple recipe can be prepared with almost any green vegetable. For a delicate touch, add 1 teaspoon of grated lemon zest, 1 tablespoon lemon juice and a few fresh sage leaves per serving. Sure to impress your mother-in-law when she drops in unexpectedly for Sunday dinner!

rotelle with cherry tomatoes and mozzarella

rotelles aux tomates cerises et à la mozzarella

5 | 10

Makes one 225g (8oz) serving

6 cherry tomatoes
1 tablespoon olive oil
1 teaspoon finely chopped garlic
½ cherry-sized mozzarella ball, cubed
55g (2oz) rotelle
3–4 fresh basil leaves, finely chopped

1. Wash the cherry tomatoes and cut them in half.
2. In a heavy-based saucepan, heat half of the olive oil over a medium heat and add the garlic. Cook for 1 minute, then add the cherry tomatoes and cook for a further 5 minutes, still over a medium heat. Remove the saucepan from the heat, add the mozzarella, return the saucepan to the heat and leave it until the mozzarella is beginning to melt.
3. Meanwhile, cook the rotelle according to the packet instructions.
4. Drain the pasta, then combine with the tomato and mozzarella mixture and sprinkle with basil.

yummy tips

If Bébé's dinner is making your partner's mouth water, cook a few slices of Parma ham in the oven (5 minutes at 240°C/475°F/Gas Mark 9). Tear into pieces and cover the ham with the rotelle, cherry tomatoes and mozzarella. A real delicacy.

fusilli with summer vegetables and basil

torsades aux légumes du soleil et basilic

5   10

Makes one 225g (8oz) serving

3 cherry tomatoes
½ courgette
¼ red pepper
1 tablespoon olive oil
1 teaspoon finely chopped garlic
3–4 fresh basil leaves, finely chopped
55g (2oz) fusilli

1. Wash the vegetables. Cut the tomatoes in half, cut the courgette first into rounds, then into quarters and cut the pepper into small pieces.
2. In a heavy-based saucepan, heat the olive oil over a medium heat and add the garlic. Cook for 1 minute, add the vegetables and basil and cook for a further 10 minutes, still over a medium heat.
3. Meanwhile, cook the pasta according to the packet instructions.
4. Drain the pasta, then mix with the vegetable sauce. If sharing with Bébé, eat while closing your eyes and dreaming of a summer evening in Provence!

yummy tips

Chop a few pitted green olives and a few slices of strong chorizo and mix them with the vegetables. Now you have a scrumptious dinner for the grown-ups.

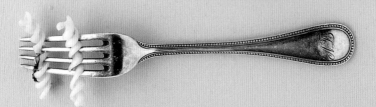

pesto penne with sugar snap peas
pennes aux pois croquants et pesto doux

5   10

Makes one 225g (8oz) serving

1 tablespoon olive oil
¼ garlic clove
5–6 fresh basil leaves
1 tablespoon pine kernels
1 tablespoon grated Parmesan
100g (3½oz) sugar snap peas or
mangetout, cut into small pieces
55g (2oz) penne

1. Using a food processor or blender, blend the olive oil, garlic, basil, pine kernels and Parmesan to a smooth pesto.
2. Bring a small pan of water to the boil and cook the sugar snap peas for 7–10 minutes.
3. Meanwhile, cook the penne according to the packet instructions.
4. Drain the pasta, then mix with the peas and pesto.

yummy tips

My daughter has fun with this dish, as she's sure that penne were made especially to fit on her little fingers! For a grown-up dish, sprinkle with shavings of fresh Parmesan and toasted pine kernels.

first trip around the world

Thanks to your tasty dishes, Bébé has become a shrewd gourmet on a quest for increasingly more intense culinary pleasures. He's curious about everything and he's more and more open to the world around him. It might be time to introduce him to the world of available flavours and help him discover foreign lands via his taste buds. At some point it became my goal to prove that it is possible to create recipes that are inspired by foreign culinary traditions while still being perfectly suitable for little ones. I believe the development of taste should be oriented towards diversity, not limited by it. The experience of cooking these meals will prove enriching for both you and Bébé. Now boarding: a gastronomic voyage with multiple stops!

INDIA

lentil dhal with coconut milk and coriander bulgar

dhal de lentilles rouges au lait de coco et boulgour à la coriandre

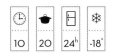

Makes five 200g (7oz) servings

For the dhal
250g (9oz) red lentils
250g (9oz) carrots
600g (1lb 5oz) tomatoes
1 tablespoon sunflower oil
½ teaspoon finely chopped garlic
1 teaspoon turmeric
½ teaspoon ground cumin
½ teaspoon ground ginger
125ml (4fl oz) vegetable stock
1 tablespoon tomato purée
250ml (9fl oz) coconut milk

For the coriander bulgar
200g (7oz) bulgar
400ml (14fl oz) water
5 fresh coriander leaves, chopped

1. Start making the dhal by rinsing the lentils, picking them over and discarding any stones or debris.
2. Put the lentils into a saucepan and cover them with twice their volume of water. Bring to the boil and cook for 10 minutes over a medium heat. Drain and set aside.
3. Wash the carrots and tomatoes. Peel the carrots and slice into thin rounds. Finely dice the tomatoes. Set aside.
4. Start the coriander bulgar by putting the bulgar and water into a pan. Bring to the boil, then lower the heat and cook for 10 minutes or until the water is completely absorbed. Remove from the heat and set aside.
5. Meanwhile, in a frying pan heat the sunflower oil over a medium heat and add the garlic. Cook for 1 minute, then add the carrots and tomatoes. Sprinkle in the spices, add the vegetable stock and tomato purée and stir well. Pour in the coconut milk, lower the heat and simmer, uncovered, for 10 minutes.
6. Blend to a smooth purée. Add the lentils and mix well.
7. Serve the dhal with the bulgar seasoned with the coriander.

yummy tips

Serving dhal to grown-ups? They will love it! Add just a pinch of cayenne pepper. Pairs well with grilled tandoori chicken.

MADE IN INDIA

SPAIN

vegetable paella

paella toute jaune aux legumes

⏰	🍲	🗄	❄
10	20	24ʰ	-18°

Makes five 200g (7oz) servings

55g (2oz) carrot
1 red pepper
1 green pepper
50g (1¾oz) green beans
1 teaspoon olive oil
1 teaspoon finely chopped shallots
Pinch of saffron (or turmeric)
½ teaspoon paprika
Pinch of salt
250g (9oz) basmati rice
55g (2oz) peas, fresh or frozen
90g (3¼oz) sweetcorn, frozen or tinned
400ml (4fl oz) water

1. Wash the vegetables. Peel and finely chop the carrot. Remove the seeds from the peppers and finely chop them as well. Cut the green beans into small pieces.
2. In a heavy-based saucepan, heat the olive oil over a medium heat and add the shallots, spices, salt and rice. Cook for 1–2 minutes, until the rice is translucent.
3. Add the chopped vegetables, peas and sweetcorn. Add the water, cover and simmer over a low heat for 15 minutes or until the water is completely absorbed.

yummy tips

You can serve this vegetable paella with a cold yogurt sauce. Simply mix several tablespoons of natural, unsweetened Greek yogurt with a pinch of cumin and a teaspoon of tomato ketchup. You can also easily transform this dish into traditional paella for you and your partner. Prepare the above recipe in a deep saucepan or wok. Add a bit of smoked paprika (depending on how spicy you like it) along with the other spices. Brown some pieces of chicken in a pan and add them to the rice when you add the water. If you are in the mood for variety, add a few tiger prawns or squid rings and some large mussels as well. To make it really special for the grown-ups, serve with a dry white wine such as a Spanish Rioja.

JAPAN

green vegetable and soba noodle stir-fry
sauté de legumes verts et nouilles soba

Makes five 200g (7oz) servings

150g (5oz) each of peas,
green beans and broccoli florets
55g (2oz) chard leaves or
fresh baby spinach leaves
200g (7oz) soba noodles,
broken into small pieces
1 tablespoon sunflower oil
½ teaspoon finely chopped garlic
1 tablespoon clear honey
1 tablespoon low-sodium soy sauce
1 tablespoon lemon juice

1. Shell the peas if using fresh. Wash the other vegetables and chop them into small pieces. Chop the chard separately.
2. Bring a pan of water to the boil and add the noodles, green beans, peas and broccoli. Boil for 3–4 minutes until the noodles are just cooked (al dente). Drain and set aside.
3. In a frying pan, heat the sunflower oil over a medium heat and add the garlic. Brown the garlic for 1 minute, then add the noodles and pre-cooked vegetables. Cook for 5 minutes, stirring frequently.
4. Add the honey, soy sauce and lemon juice as well as the chard and cook for a further 2 minutes. Serve warm in Bébé's favourite bowl.

yummy tips

Add 200g (7oz) thinly sliced sirloin steak and a pinch of cayenne pepper to this stir-fry and you'll have a tasty and healthy supper for grown-ups!

THAILAND
mild vegetable curry with thai rice
curry tout doux de legumes et riz thaï

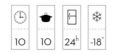

Makes five 200g (7oz) servings

300g (10½oz) sweet potato
100g (3½oz) carrots
175g (6oz) pumpkin or butternut squash
½ yellow pepper
1 teaspoon sunflower oil
½ teaspoon finely chopped garlic
250ml (9fl oz) coconut milk
1 teaspoon lime juice
1 teaspoon soft brown sugar
½ teaspoon ground ginger
4–5 fresh coriander leaves
Pinch of salt
150g (5oz) Thai rice

1. Wash the vegetables, then peel and chop them into small pieces. Bring a pan of water to the boil and add the vegetables. Cook for 5 minutes, drain and set aside.
2. In a heavy-based saucepan, heat the oil over a medium heat and add the garlic. Brown for 1 minute and add the vegetables, coconut milk, lime juice, brown sugar, ginger, coriander and salt. Cover and simmer for 10 minutes.
3. Meanwhile, prepare the rice according to the packet instructions.
4. Serve the vegetable curry with the rice.

yummy tips
For variety you can use different vegetables in this recipe. Firm vegetables or root vegetables work best. A pinch of chilli pepper and grated fresh root ginger turns this dish into a delight for grown-ups.

Chiara, 20 months

Vera, 16 months

big kid snacks & treats

for kids from 1 to 99

muesli crumbles

Crispy and crunchy on top, soft and gooey underneath: beyond the health benefits of the whole grains and fresh fruit (full of vitamins, fibre and minerals) they contain, these muesli crumbles are a veritable mine of gustatory exploration – and pleasure too! – for little ones. These 'big kid snacks' are easy to eat: Bébé can peck at the pieces of crunchy crumble and pop the pieces of softened fruit into her mouth with her little fingers. I make them in disposable muffin cases; paper cases if I want to reheat them in the microwave or foil if they will be served cold at a picnic. For an extra treat, add a big scoop of vanilla ice cream on the side of Bébé's dish and take care nobody tries to steal it away from her!

banana-mango muesli crumbles
muesli-crumble bananes et mangues

5 | 15

Makes 6–12 treats

6 standard (or 12 mini-) muffin cases
2 bananas
12 slices frozen peeled mango
250g (9oz) muesli with raisins
25g (1oz) tablespoons butter
1 teaspoon clear honey

1. Preheat the oven to 220°C (425°F/Gas Mark 7).
2. Line a muffin tin, mini-muffin tin or baking tray with the muffin cases.
3. Peel the bananas and slice them into rounds.
4. Distribute the slices of frozen mango among the muffin cases and add the banana slices on top.
5. Cover the fruit with the muesli and add a few small knobs of butter and 1–2 drops of honey to each crumble.
6. Bake for 15 minutes. Take care the crumble doesn't brown too much. You can cover the muffin tins with foil for the final minutes, if needed.
7. Remove the crumbles from the oven and leave to cool. Serve warm or once cool, put them into a freezer bag and freeze.

yummy tips
This tropical fruit crumble can be made with pineapple or lychees instead of mango.

yellow plum and chocolate muesli crumbles
muesli-crumble mirabelles et chocolat

5   15

Makes 6–12 treats

6 standard (or 12 mini-) muffin cases
1kg (2lb 4oz) yellow (Mirabelle) plums
1 tablespoon soft brown sugar
250g (9oz) crunchy chocolate
chip muesli
25g (1oz) tablespoons butter
1 teaspoon clear honey

1. Preheat the oven to 220°C (425°F/Gas Mark 7).
2. Line a muffin tin, mini-muffin tin or baking tray with the muffin cases.
3. Wash and stone the plums, then cut them into quarters.
4. Distribute the plums among the muffin cases and sprinkle with the sugar.
5. Cover the fruit with the crunchy chocolate chip muesli and add a few small knobs of butter and 1–2 drops of honey to each crumble.
6. Bake for 15 minutes. Take care the crumble doesn't brown too much. You can cover the muffin tins with foil for the final minutes, if needed.
7. Remove the crumbles from the oven and leave to cool. Serve warm or once cool, put them into a freezer bag and freeze.

yummy tips

Can't find crunchy chocolate chip muesli? If you don't want to miss out on the chocolate, simply chop a few squares of your favourite chocolate and add it to the muesli.

raspberry-mint muesli crumbles
muesli-crumble framboises et menthe

5 | 15

Makes 6–12 treats

6 standard (or 12 mini-) muffin cases
450g (1lb) raspberries
1 tablespoon soft brown sugar
6 fresh mint leaves
250g (9oz) crunchy muesli with dried fruit
25g (1oz) tablespoons butter
1 teaspoon clear honey

1. Preheat the oven to 220°C (425°F/Gas Mark 7).
2. Line a muffin tin, mini-muffin tin or baking tray with the muffin cases.
3. Wash the raspberries well and distribute among the muffin cases. Sprinkle with the sugar. Finely chop the mint leaves and sprinkle them over the raspberries.
4. Cover the fruit with the crunchy muesli and add a few small knobs of butter and 1–2 drops of honey to each.
5. Bake for 15 minutes. Take care the crumble doesn't brown too much. You can cover the muffin tins with foil for the final minutes if needed.
6. Remove the crumbles from the oven and leave to cool. Serve warm or once cool, put them into a freezer bag and freeze.

yummy tips

You can also make this recipe with strawberries or blueberries when they're in season. For a quick dessert (no cooking required), fill small glasses with a layer of fruit, then fromage frais or natural, unsweetened Greek yogurt, a couple of drops of clear honey and crunchy muesli on top. Quick, attractive and, above all, delicious!

melon-peach kebabs
brochettes melon-pêche

Makes 2 treats

5

2 slices melon
1 yellow peach
2 wooden skewers

1. Peel and deseed the melon, then cut it into
small cubes.
2. Wash the peach and remove the stone, then cut it
into small pieces.
3. Slide the fruit on to wooden skewers, alternating
melon cubes and peach pieces.
4. Before serving the kebabs to Bébé use scissors to
cut off the sharp tips of the skewers.

strawberry-raspberry kebabs
brochettes fraise-framboise

Makes 2 treats

5

5 strawberries
10 large raspberries
2 wooden skewers

1. Wash the strawberries well, remove any stalks and
cut them in half.
2. Wash the raspberries well, inside and out.
3. Slide the berries on to wooden skewers,
alternating strawberries and raspberries.
4. Before serving the kebabs to Bébé use scissors to
cut off the sharp tips of the skewers.

mango-banana kebabs
brochettes mangue-banane

Makes 2 treats

5

½ mango
1 banana
2 wooden skewers

1. Without breaking through the peel, score the flesh of the half mango first lengthways and then widthways. Invert the mango half by pressing the peel side in, then slide the knife along the peel to remove the mango cubes that are now sticking up.
2. Peel the banana and slice it into rounds.
3. Slide the fruit on to wooden skewers, alternating cubes and rounds. Before serving the kebabs to Bébé use scissors to cut off the sharp tips of the skewers.

clementine-grape kebabs
brochettes raisin-clémentine

Makes 2 treats

5

10 seedless green grapes
1 clementine
2 wooden skewers

1. Wash the grapes and cut them in half.
2. Peel the clementine and remove as much of the white pith as possible. Separate the sections.
3. Slide the fruit on to wooden skewers, alternating grapes and sections of clementine. Before serving the kebabs to Bébé use scissors to cut off the sharp tips of the skewers.

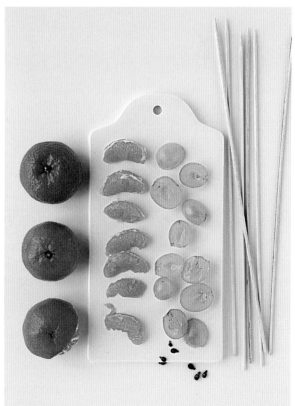

lemon-yogurt cake
gateau au citron et au yaourt

10   45

Serves 8–10

125ml (4fl oz) natural,
unsweetened Greek yogurt
200g (7oz) caster sugar
1 vanilla pod
2 eggs
50g (1¾oz) butter, melted
Pinch of salt
250g (9oz) plain flour
Juice from 1 lemon

1. Preheat the oven to 180°C (350°F/Gas Mark 4).
2. Mix the yogurt and sugar in a bowl.
3. With a knife, open the vanilla pod lengthways and scrape out the seeds into the bowl.
4. Break the eggs into the yogurt mixture and beat them in vigorously.
5. Add the butter and salt and mix. Then add the flour in small amounts, stirring each time until the batter is smooth. Stir in the lemon juice.
6. Pour the cake batter into a 25-cm (10-inch) silicone mould or buttered cake tin. Bake for 45 minutes.
7. Check that the cake is cooked by inserting a skewer into its centre; if the skewer comes out clean, the cake is ready.
8. Leave it to sit for a few minutes before removing it from the cake tin.
9. Serve the cake warm with a fruit kebab!

yummy tips

Try variants of this cake by replacing the lemon juice with 15g (½oz) of cocoa powder, the juice of ½ an orange or 100g (3½oz) frozen raspberries.

Maya's mini-muffins
les mini-muffins de Maya

10   15

Makes 20 mini-muffins

20 mini-muffin cases
4 eggs
250g (9oz) caster sugar
1 vanilla pod
6 tablespoons water
2 teaspoons plus a pinch
of bicarbonate of soda
250g (9oz) plain flour

1. Preheat the oven to 180°C (350°F/Gas Mark 4).
2. Line a mini-muffin tin or baking sheet with the cases.
3. Break the eggs into a bowl and add the sugar. Beat vigorously.
4. With a knife, open the vanilla pod lengthways and scrape out the seeds into the bowl.
5. Add the water and continue to beat the mixture. Add the bicarbonate of soda, then incorporate the flour gradually, mixing constantly.
6. Half-fill the muffin cases with batter. Bake for 15 minutes.
7. Check that the mini-muffins are done by sticking a skewer into their centre. If the skewer comes out clean, the muffins are ready.
8. Remove the muffins from oven and leave them to cool on a rack before you serve them with fruit kebabs.

yummy tips

You can turn these kids' mini-muffins into light *financiers* by adding 50g (1¾oz) ground almonds in with the flour. Very, very enjoyable, but only recommended for babies older than six months and with no family history of food allergies.

oatmeal biscuits
biscuits aux flocons d'avoine

Makes 16–20 biscuits

115g (4oz) butter
250g (9oz) porridge oats
150g (5oz) soft brown sugar
100g (3½oz) raisins
150g (5oz) plain flour
5 tablespoons water

1. Preheat the oven to 180°C (350°F/Gas Mark 4).
2. Melt the butter.
3. Put the oats into a mixing bowl, then pour the melted butter over them and stir.
4. Add the sugar and raisins, then incorporate the flour gradually. Mix in the water. Your mixture should be firm.
5. Make small balls of biscuit mixture and place them 5cm (2inches) apart on a baking tray lined with baking parchment. Flatten them slightly and bake in the centre of the oven for 10 minutes.
6. Remove the biscuits from the oven and leave them to cool on a rack before serving with fruit kebabs.

yummy tips

Feeling naughty? Replace the raisins with chocolate chips …
Shhh! We won't tell Dr Lalau Keraly!

milkshakes: the basics ...

milk-shake: la base ...

24ʰ   -18°

Makes two 150ml
(5fl oz) servings

125ml (4fl oz) natural, unsweetened
Greek yogurt
125ml (4fl oz) full-fat milk

strawberries and a pinch of soft brown sugar

6–8 strawberries, washed well and stalks removed
1 teaspoon soft brown sugar

mango and banana

½ mango, peeled and stoned
½ banana with skin removed

blueberries and raspberries

2 tablespoons blueberries, washed well
10 raspberries, washed well

peach and a drop of honey

1 peach, stoned and peeled
1 teaspoon clear honey

1. Put the yogurt, milk and fruit into a bowl, as well as any sugar or honey (if you're serving to children twelve months and over).
2. Blend well until there are no lumps.
3. If the milkshake is too thick, add a bit more milk and stir.

fruit toasties

Because there is nothing more satisfying than a child taking immense pleasure from a meal, I came up with these fruit toasties, which elicited a hip-hip-hooray from my children and their friends. The most fabulous thing about these fruity snacks is, of course, that they are fun. Obviously, these toasties are full of the nutritional benefits of fresh fruit, which helps your child fill up on vitamins, minerals and fibre. But at this exploratory stage when Bébé begins to enjoy seeing familiar objects appear and reappear, watching her plate become a hide-and-seek playground will be an unmatchable pleasure for her. And if she manages to hold these little fruit toasties in her own little foodie hands, the bonus is another step towards independence. Everything about these snacks is good!

basic recipe
recette de base

🕐	🍲	🧊	❄
5	3	24ʰ	-18°

Makes 1 fruit toastie

2 slices brown or granary bread
½ teaspoon butter
One of the fruit fillings
on the following pages

1. Butter the slices of bread on one side.
2. Spread the fruit filling (see recipes on the following pages) on the buttered side of one of the slices and cover with the other slice, buttered side towards the fruit.
3. Place the fruit toastie under a preheated hot grill and cook for about 3–5 minutes, turning halfway through.
4. Remove the fruit toastie from the grill and leave to cool before cutting diagonally in half.
5. Bébé can eat these fruit toasties all on her own at home, at a picnic, on the road ... it's the most practical snack ever!

yummy tips

When you bring your favourite fruit toasties on a picnic with you, leave them to cool entirely before wrapping them in foil. And don't cut them in half or the fruit will ooze out before snack time! These will keep for a couple of hours in a polythene bag.

apple-banana filling
garniture pomme-banane

½ apple
½ banana

5 · 3

24ʰ · −18°

1. Wash the apple and remove the core and any spare pips. Grate the apple and squeeze the pulp between your hands to remove some of the juice, which would otherwise make the fruit toastie soggy.
2. Peel the banana and slice it into rounds.
3. Place the grated apple and the banana slices on a slice of buttered bread, cover with the other slice and cook according to the basic recipe.

mango-lychee filling
garniture mangue-litchi

4 slices mango
3 lychees, peeled and stoned

5 · 3

24ʰ · −18°

1. Cut the stoned lychees into quarters and place them on kitchen paper for a few minutes to absorb some of their juice. Wet fruit will result in a soggy fruit toastie.
2. Place the slices of mango and the lychees on a slice of buttered bread, cover with the other slice and cook according to the basic recipe.

vanilla-pear filling
garniture poire-vanille

½ pear
1 vanilla pod

5 | 3

24ʰ | -18°

1. Wash the pear and remove the core and any spare pips. Store one half of the pear in cling film in the refrigerator. Slice the other half into thin slices.
2. With a knife, open the vanilla pod lengthways and scrape out the seeds.
3. Place the pear slices and the vanilla pod seeds on a slice of buttered bread, cover with the other slice of bread and cook according to the basic recipe.

fig and honey filling
garniture figue au miel

1 very ripe fig
1 teaspoon clear honey

5 | 3

24ʰ | -18°

1. Cut the fig in half and scrape out all of the red pulp. Discard the skin.
2. Spread the fig pulp on a slice of buttered bread, add the honey, cover with the other slice of bread and cook according to the basic recipe.

first birthday

Pfffffftttt! In a spray of spittle, Bébé is already blowing out her first candle. Along with her first teeth, her first words and her first steps, this is a marvellous moment. And just because she's only twelve months old doesn't mean she has to stick to her usual apple-banana compote! At one year, you can serve her a real big kid birthday treat. Because once in a while it's great to indulge in something exceptional – and to do so as a family. So here is my favourite selection of *crème de la crème* birthday cakes for 'big bébé gourmets'! They have brought joy to my daughter's, son's, nieces' and nephews' birthday parties … and to their respective parents. Get ready for sticky faces and hands!

my grandmother's birthday cake
gateau d'anniversaire de ma grand-mère

10 | **45**

Serves 8–10

For the sponge cake

4 eggs

250g (9oz) caster sugar

1 vanilla pod

6 tablespoons water

2 teaspoons plus a pinch of bicarbonate of soda

250g (9oz) plain flour

For the icing

2 vanilla pods

400ml (14fl oz) double cream

1 teaspoon vanilla extract

1½ teaspoons caster sugar

115g (4oz) raspberry or strawberry jam

450g (1lb) raspberries, washed well

And one magnificent birthday candle!

1. Preheat the oven to 180°C (350°F/Gas Mark 4).
2. Break the eggs into a bowl and add the sugar. With a knife, open the vanilla pod lengthways and scrape out the seeds into the bowl. Beat well. Add the water and continue to beat the mixture. Add the bicarbonate of soda and incorporate the flour gradually.
3. Pour the batter into a buttered 25-cm (10-inch) round cake tin. Bake in the preheated oven for 45 minutes. Check that the sponge cake is cooked through by inserting a skewer into the centre; if the skewer comes out clean, the cake is done. Leave the cake to cool in the tin, then transfer it to a wire rack.
4. Next, prepare the icing. With a knife, open the vanilla pods lengthways and scrape out the seeds.
5. Put the cream, vanilla extract, sugar and vanilla pod seeds into a bowl. Whip this mixture until it forms stiff peaks. (I advise using an electric whisk.) Leave it to sit in the refrigerator for 30 minutes.
6. When the sponge cake has cooled completely, cut it horizontally into 3 rounds, each about 1.25cm (½ inch) thick.
7. Take the top round, turn it over and place it on a serving dish or large plate. Spread 2 tablespoons of jam on top (cut side), add a layer of vanilla whipped cream, then half of the fresh raspberries. Place the second sponge cake round on top and repeat the previous step, reserving 9 raspberries for the top. Finish with the last sponge cake round.
8. Cover the cake entirely with the remaining whipped cream and decorate with the reserved fresh raspberries and the birthday candle. Leave to sit for 1 hour before serving.

chocolate-covered dried fruit treats
bonbons de fruits secs en robe de chocolat

15 | 5

Makes 20 treats

20 mini-muffin cases
10 ready-to-eat dried apricots
55g (2oz) raisins
4 prunes
100g (3½oz) milk chocolate

1. Place the muffin cases on a tray.
2. Chop the dried fruit.
3. Place the chocolate in a heatproof bowl over a saucepan of simmering water (do not allow the base of the bowl to touch the water) and allow the chocolate to melt, stirring gently from time to time (no water should spill into the chocolate).
4. Once the chocolate is melted, add the dried fruit. Mix well, until all the fruit is covered with chocolate.
5. Using 2 teaspoons, drop a small amount of chocolate-covered fruit into each muffin case.
6. Place the tray immediately into the refrigerator and leave the treats to chill for 2 hours before serving.

yummy tips

These treats are so easy to make. I frequently make an adult version by adding chopped hazelnuts and using dark chocolate. They're perfect with coffee after a nice meal and much more nutritious than an ordinary chocolate truffle.

caramel-covered fresh fruit lollipops
sucettes de fruits frais au caramel

10 | 5

Makes 20 lollipops

20 wooden skewers
20 strawberries
3 sweet-tart apples
(Royal Gala, Pink Lady)
250g (9oz) caster sugar
150ml (5fl oz) water

1. Use scissors to cut off the sharp ends of the skewers and cover a dish with baking parchment.
2. Wash the strawberries and remove any leaves. Wash the apples, remove the cores and any spare pips and cut into small cubes. Slide a strawberry and two apple cubes on to a wooden skewer.
3. Now get any children out of the kitchen. You are going to make caramel and it's very, very hot! Pour the sugar and water into a saucepan. Bring to the boil without stirring. When the sugar begins to brown, stir delicately. As soon as the caramel is golden in colour, remove the saucepan from the heat and set it in cold water to stop the caramelisation.
4. Caramel solidifies rapidly, so don't waste any time: dip your fresh fruit lollipops one by one into the caramel. Lay them on the dish covered in baking parchment to cool and harden.
5. Once cool, arrange the lollipops in a vase or a sturdy glass and let the children help themselves to these crunchy, fruity lollipops.

yummy tips
You can make these lollipops using any firm and slightly tart fruit. Forget about bananas, but melon, nectarines and apricots work well.

raspberry roll
roulé aux framboises

10   8

Serves 10

3 eggs
200g (7oz) caster sugar
2 teaspoons plus a pinch of
bicarbonate of soda
200g (7oz) plain flour
4 tablespoons full-fat milk
450g (1lb) raspberries, washed well
and crushed

1. Preheat the oven to 200°C (400°F/Gas Mark 6) and line a Swiss roll tin or rectangular 30 x 40-cm (10½ x 15½-inch) ovenproof dish with baking parchment.
2. Break the eggs into a bowl and add the sugar. Beat with an electric whisk until light and airy.
3. Stirring constantly, add the bicarbonate of soda and flour. Pour in the milk and whip lightly until the batter is smooth.
4. Pour the batter into the tin. Bake in the preheated oven for 8–10 minutes. It should be springy to the touch and beginning to shrink away from the sides of the tin.
5. Remove the sponge cake from the oven and turn it out on to baking parchment on your work surface. Spread the crushed raspberries evenly over the surface and, starting with the short side, roll the cake until you have a formed a Swiss roll.
6. Place the roll in the refrigerator with the join underneath. Leave it to sit for 1 hour.
7. Cut the roll into 2-cm (¾-inch) slices and serve!

yummy tips

No fresh fruit in the refrigerator? In lieu of raspberries, you can fill your roll with any thick compote, such as those on pages 24–35.

frequently asked questions
with Dr Jean Lalau Keraly
& nutritional information

FAQ with Dr Jean Lalau Keraly

fruit

I peel all fruit. Is this best for my baby?
Let's not forget that the vitamins and minerals in fruit are found in high concentrations in and under the skin. By removing the skin and outer layer of pulp with a knife, 25 per cent of the benefits of these nutrients are lost. I recommend using only organic fruit or fruit that has not been treated after harvest, because pesticides stay on the skin. Always thoroughly wash fruit before eating it. And if the outermost layer is decidedly unappealing to you, scrape it off lightly with a sharp knife in order to preserve as much of the fruit's nutritional value as possible.

Some compotes are raw. Can my baby eat them?
When your baby first begins to eat solid foods, I suggest caution with raw fruit because it can be more difficult to digest than cooked fruit. However, once your baby is accostumed to her first purees, she can indulge in ripe, raw fruit, which abounds with nutritional and sensorial benefits. What a giant step it is, in learning the pleasures of eating, for your baby to grip juicy slices of peach or melon to taste, suckle and munch at will.

Fruit before bed – is that such a good idea?
You must be thinking of the recommendation to avoid giving children sugary foods in the evening because sugar (glucose) is a stimulant incompatible with bedtime. However, the sugar in fruit (fructose) is different from processed sugar and doesn't have the same disadvantages as the glucose found in sweets. On the contrary, I think, it even stimulates digestion – perfect for a good night's sleep!

Should I sweeten my baby's yogurt with honey rather than caster sugar?
Once your baby is one year old, yes! Not only does it take less honey than caster sugar to sweeten a serving of yogurt, clear honey is sweeter than caster sugar and has fewer calories per teaspoon. However, honey can contain bacteria that can lead to botulism, a very serious illness, in children under 12 months old, so don't give it to them.

If I mix fresh fruit and dairy, won't it be difficult for my baby to digest?
You must be referring to the notion that dairy and raw fruit can curdle and, therefore, the idea of giving Baby the two combined feels risky. No problem. Baby formula is specially adapted to your child's needs. From six months on, blended raw fruit is perfectly suitable for babies.

Can apricot compote give my baby a tummy ache?
Apricots are slightly acidic, but if they are nice and ripe, there is no reason to worry for your little one. Apricots are among the first fruits intro-

duced to an infant's diet because they are easy on the tummy. And apricot fibres are soft and well tolerated by the fragile intestines of an infant.

What is the nutritional value of dried apricots for my baby?

Dried apricots – like all dried fruit – are rich in fibre and trace elements. They contain five times more carbohydrates than fresh apricots, which make them an ideal snack when you need an energy boost. They are also rich in beta-carotene, potassium and iron and have antioxidant and anti-anaemic qualities.

Are tropical fruits allergenic?

Long live tropical fruits! Contrary to what was commonly believed for many years, recent studies show that tropical fruits are no more likely than other fruits to cause food allergies. And they have the advantage of being available in winter when other fruits are out of season. Apart from their rich vitamin content, they go well in sweet and savoury dishes, which is ideal for introducing little ones to new recipes.

Isn't banana-mango compote a little exotic for an infant?

Exotic, perhaps, but from whose point of view? For an Ecuadorian infant, an apple-pear compote would be exotic. Mangoes and bananas are excellent first fruits to introduce and they're no more allergenic than common fruit. Pineapple, however, should probably come later, not because it is allergenic but because of its fibrous texture.

I'm allergic to raspberries. Should I avoid giving them to my baby as well?

We often confuse food allergies with food intolerances. Very few people have a real food allergy, which in the 30 minutes following ingestion brings on a violent allergic reaction, such as swelling, vomiting or difficulty breathing. It is possible to have an intolerance for a certain food at one point in time, without ever having a problem after that. The opposite is also true. Raspberries are histamine liberators. Occasionally, susceptable people find that these foods may induce a peak release of histamines that can cause a rash, for example. However, this is not the same as a real food allergy, and your baby may not have any problem with raspberries. Simply introduce this food slowly. If all goes well, there's no need to deprive your baby.

Can blueberries be allergenic?

Blueberries, as their name implies, are berries and thus subject to berries' reputation of being allergenic. However, many studies have found that unless your child has a history of allergies, berries are no more allergenic for infants than other common fruits. You can therefore give your baby blueberries without fear. Just make sure you introduce them into the diet gradually in small amounts. Introduce new foods one at a time, so if there is a reaction you know which food has triggered it.

vegetables

Shouldn't I always peel the vegetables I feed to my baby?

You certainly can peel the vegetables you feed to your baby, but bear this in mind: just as with fruit, much of the vitamins contained in vegetables are concentrated in their skin and just underneath. It would be a shame to forgo so many of the nutritional benefits of your vegetables by removing their thick outer layer. If your baby doesn't like the skin, you can either blend your purée more finely or lightly scrape the vegetables with a sharp knife to remove just a thin layer, preserving as many vitamins as possible.

Isn't it best to steam vegetables?

Better yet, cook your vegetables in a pan with a small amount of water at the base. Not only is this technique quicker than steaming or boiling, but the water left over from cooking can be incorporated into the purée. Why would you want to do that? Because during cooking some of the vitamins dissolve into the water. By using the water to mix the purée, you enrich the already nutritious purée further.Your baby will feast on a vegetable dish full of vitamins and minerals.

I've heard that certain vegetables contain nitrates. Is this true?

Yes and no. Vegetables with high nitrate content include leafy greens such as spinach and endive. Tomatoes, mushrooms and peas are low in nitrates, while green beans are somewhere in between. As much as possible, use organic or fresh vegetables (which are often less rich in nitrates) for your purées. That said, let's clarify. Nitrates themselves pose no health risk. It's nitrites (modified nitrates) that do. It is nearly impossible to be contaminated by vegetables treated with nitrates. However, the danger lies in the vegetable purée that has been sitting in the fridge for more than 24 hours and whose nitrates have had time to transform into nitrites. For infants younger than twelve months, I recommend that vegetable dishes are eaten straightaway or frozen as soon as they are cooled.

There are always lots of potatoes in bottles of commercial baby food. Will my baby really like 'pure' purées?

You bring up an interesting point here: the systematic addition of potatoes to most shop-bought baby food. While potatoes are wonderful with a touch of butter, don't forget that they are not vegetables but starch and as such are less rich in vitamins but much richer in carbohydrates. I might add that their neutral flavour does nothing to develop the flavour palate of your child. If manufacturers use large amounts of potato in their recipes, it's in part to dull the taste of some flavourful vegetables, thus contributing to the homogenisation of food in our culture, but more important, it's because potatoes are cheaper than 'real' vegetables. Therefore, on the contrary, serving your baby 'pure' purée has nutritional benefits and encourages the discovery of new flavours.

What's all this about parsnips?

Indeed, few people are familiar with this 'forgotten' vegetable, whose heyday was from antiquity through the Middle Ages. A member of the carrot family, the parsnip was a staple food source, especially in north-eastern Europe. The parsnip is still popular in those regions, thanks to its nutritional value. Parsnips are rich in fibre and help fight constipation. Look for smaller, more tender parsnips because they cook more quickly, which is helpful when Baby is howling for the next meal!

Why should I use sweet potatoes instead of potatoes? Aren't they allergenic?

Sweet potatoes are comparatively low in calories, have a higher nutrient content than white potatoes and are just as easy to prepare. And their slightly sweet flavour is pleasant and comforting for little mouths. Sweet potatoes are a tuber and have little allergic potential for infants.

But what's wrong with good old-fashioned mashed potatoes?

While potatoes shouldn't be eliminated entirely from the infant diet, remember that they have less nutritional value than other vegetables. Our culture today favours starchy foods such as rice, potatoes, bread and pasta. Our role – and yours, as a parent – is to help your baby learn to eat 'real' vegetables, in purées and then in whole pieces. Not to mention that swedes and celeriac are much more flavourful than the rather neutral-tasting potato.

Should I serve pumpkin to my baby?

Pumpkin and other squash, such as butternut, are not only rich nutritionally speaking, but also have a lovely nutty flavour. They are a great source of vitamins, as well as trace elements such as phosphorus, magnesium and potassium. Pumpkin contains good amounts of carotene (twice as much as in carrots), which is excellent for your baby's skin.

Can peas give my baby a tummy ache?

Yes and no. When solid foods are first introduced, a baby's digestive tract may not yet be mature enough to handle fibrous or gas-producing vegetables such as peas or cabbage. But it's just a matter of time. Once your baby is well accustomed to solid foods, peas will no longer be difficult to digest.

Will cauliflower make my baby colicky?

It's not the cauliflower itself but the sulphur – a trace element it contains that makes this delicious vegetable sometimes difficult to digest. To ward off bloating, change the water in your pan partway through cooking (much of the sulphur will go out with the first round of water). When your baby is over eight months old, add a few grains of cumin or fennel seeds to your mixture. These spices help combat wind.

I've heard that peppers aren't good for babies. Is this true?

Peppers are, indeed, difficult to digest when eaten raw and unpeeled, hence the rumour that they are not a good food for infants. However, once peppers are cooked, peeled and deseeded, they are perfectly suitable for all. Considering how beneficial peppers can be, it would be a shame to leave them out of your baby's diet. However, it's a good idea to wait to add them until solid foods have been well integrated. When your baby is eight to nine months old you can start to work the peppers in.

Do tomatoes have better nutritional value raw or cooked?

Either cooked or raw, tomatoes are full of nutritional benefits, thanks to high doses of vitamin C (found in the viscous casing of their seeds), potassium and folic acid, and they are low in calories. However, it is true that cooked tomatoes – including sauces and concentrates – are richer than raw tomatoes in the carotenoid 'lycopene', a powerful antioxidant.

Won't broad beans give my baby wind?

Broad beans are indeed very rich in fibre, which activates the bowel and facilitates movement through the intestine. This increased activity can sometimes irritate an infant's fragile intestine. Bear in mind that most of the fibre in the beans is contained in their outermost skin. To eliminate much of the fibre, you can simply remove the first skin of the bean or purchase frozen broad beans without the skins.

Favism (G6PD deficiency), an extremely rare disease, is said to be linked to broad beans. Why risk feeding them to my baby?
Broad beans are not the cause of this hereditary disease, but their consumption can sometimes spark symptoms (destruction of red blood cells) in carriers of a certain chromosomal mutation. This disease is mainly found in families of Mediterranean origin. If this disease has occurred within your family, ask your GP for advice.

Is sweetcorn suitable for babies?
Not only is sweetcorn full of nutrients, it is gluten-free. This is good news for children with allergies. Sweetcorn is thus a strong candidate for the top ten super-star foods for babies!

Shouldn't I be worried about genetically modified sweetcorn?
Indeed, we should be careful about what foods we eat and those we feed to our children. Check the label on the sweetcorn products you buy (fresh, frozen, tinned, syrup) and make sure that it says 'No GMOs'. Better yet, buy only organic sweetcorn products.

Can I serve my baby shop-bought ratatouille and other dishes if I don't have time to cook?
Beware of dishes you don't make yourself, as they can contain large amounts of extra salt and fat. While these ingredients make dishes more appetising for adults, they are unsuitable in large quantities for your baby. In addition, such dishes tend to contain artificial colouring and preservatives,

which are not generally found in baby food. If you are really short on time, read the list of ingredients carefully and try to choose dishes with as few additives (including salt and fat) as possible.

I've never heard of red lentils before. Why should I serve them to my baby?
The differences among varieties of lentils are subtle. All lentils are rich in proteins and fibre. Red lentils, in addition to their lovely colour, are tender and thus have a shorter cooking time than their green or Puy cousins. That's a clear advantage when every minute counts.

meat

Isn't pork just a fatty meat?
Away with misconceptions! Pork is no fattier than other meats. On average, a portion of lean pork has about the same number of calories as a portion of chicken, which is reputed to be a lean meat. In addition, most of the fat found in pork is composed of unsaturated fatty acids, which are helpful in preventing cardiovascular disease. Finally, pork is a good source of high-quality proteins. An average portion of pork covers half of an adult's daily protein needs. Beware, however, of sausage, bacon, ribs and other pork products that are indeed high in salt and fat.

Will my baby like the taste of lamb? I personally find the taste too strong.
Taste and colour are linked to personal preference. But just because you don't like lamb doesn't mean your child won't. Give him a chance to try it, for the sake of the nutritional benefits lamb has to offer. A side dish of Carrot and Cumin Purée (page 67) might be a nice addition. And bear in mind

that all tastes are acquired. You may not think you like lamb, but you might be surprised to find you enjoy the recipes in this book.

fish and shellfish

Is it absolutely necessary for my baby to eat fish?

From six to seven months on, your baby will need sources of protein other than milk. Fish is very good in this role. Many types contain omega-3, which plays a crucial role in sight and brain development. Indeed, a child's brain continues to grow until it reaches the size of an adult brain, around five years of age. It is easy to see that eating fish can be extremely beneficial for your little one.

Isn't the flavour of salmon too strong for an infant?

Why be afraid of introducing your baby to strong flavours? The wider the range of tastes your baby gets accustomed to, the better he will be prepared to enjoy the diversity of food later on. If your baby doesn't like the taste of salmon the first time, don't be discouraged. Try it again at a later date.

I avoid tuna for environmental reasons. What can I replace it with? Is my baby missing out on a superfood?

It's true, nutritional value among the different kinds of fish varies some, but there are nonetheless important similarities. It's fish itself that is a superfood, with a miraculously low lipid content (often plenty of omega-3) and a protein content equal to that of meat – not to mention the phosphorus, magnesium and iodine fish contains. You can therefore easily replace tuna with cod or salmon, for example.

When can my baby start eating prawns?

In general, the addition of crustaceans such as prawns to your baby's diet should be done with care, and families with a history of food allergies may want to check with their doctor. Indeed, crustaceans can provoke severe allergic reactions – as can peanuts and kiwis – such as eczema or anaphylactic shock. If all other solid foods have been well tolerated by your child, there is no reason why you shouldn't add prawns at six months. However, it is a good idea to give very small quantities at first so that you can observe your child's reaction in the minutes, hours and days that follow. If all goes well, you can serve Jenny's Vegetable Paella (page 138) with prawns!

starches

What is bulgar?

Originally found in the Balkan region, bulgar is made of parboiled wheat that is then dried, husked and more or less finely crushed. Bulgar is a good source of B vitamins. This starch also contains minerals such as iron, and is a good source of fibre. Finally, it's easy to digest and quick to prepare, a useful advantage when you're in a hurry to feed Baby.

What are soba noodles? Are they good for my baby?

Soba noodles are made from wholewheat and buckwheat flour. While its name can be misleading, buckwheat is not actually a variety of wheat. Gluten-free and easy to digest, pure buckwheat is suitable for people with an intolerance to gluten or who are subject to colic. Furthermore, a Canadian study has shown a favourable effect of buckwheat on blood sugar levels, which is good news for diabetics. Not to mention that buckwheat is a good source of minerals, such as fortifying phosphorus. Finally, in Japanese culture, soba noodles are eaten at the New Year to ensure a long life.

Won't so much rice in the evening before bed constipate my child?

In children who frequently eat rice, the constipation culprit is the lack of natural fibres found in vegetables and fruits, not the rice. Rice is an excellent starch that's rich in minerals and vitamin B5. A dish of rice and stewed mixed vegetables is a nutritious meal that is ideal for your child's digestive system. If constipation is a problem for your child, choose wholegrain rice, which is rich in fibre and will help prevent bowel sluggishness.

cheese

Isn't ricotta one of the cheeses that harbours dangerous bacteria?

You are probably thinking of listeria, a bacteria that can develop in raw-milk cheeses, dried meats and sausages and foods for which the cold chain can be compromised between manufacturer and retail shop. Listeria can indeed cause serious infections in very young infants. However, it is not a problem in fresh, soft cheeses made with pasteurised milk, like ricotta.

Isn't Parmesan too salty for my baby?

You are right: salt should not be added to your little one's diet, not until at least two years of age. But the goal is not to eliminate all natural sources of salt, which is beneficial for your child. A baby is simply not able to eliminate a lot of excess salt, which is why the salt naturally found in vegetables and other foods is sufficient for her. This is why paediatricians say and repeat, that you should not add salt to your infant's food. The salt in Parmesan will naturally season the dish, so you don't have to add any more than that.

sweets

Am I encouraging a junk food diet if I give my child biscuits?

It's true, we hear a lot about the overconsumption of sugary (and greasy) foods, especially in children and the facts are there. But try to remain level-headed and keep from giving in to paranoia. A little biscuit from time to time never made a child obese. Especially not a home-made biscuit. You can control its ingredients and how much sugar and fat go into it. The less processed food (rich in hidden sugars, fats and salt) your child eats, the better prepared he will be as an adult to maintain a balanced diet.

Shouldn't I think twice about giving my baby sweets?

There are sweets and there are *sweets*. If we're talking about industrial sweets full of processed sugar, you should keep your children as far away as possible from these 'foods' that provide them with nothing but cavities. In this book we include good sweets, little treats to make your baby happy or to make it a special day. But they're healthy, too. Raisins and oatmeal biscuits are filled with good things. The natural sweets in this book are soft and easy to eat. So you can give your baby a piece to taste and know that it's safe.

spices

Isn't there a chance my baby could be allergic to cinnamon or cumin?

Don't worry: cinnamon and cumin (and mild spices in general) are unlikely to pose a health risk for infants over the age of eight months – on the contrary! Cinnamon stimulates your baby's taste buds and offers an opportunity to learn a new flavour.

I would advise sticking to real Ceylon cinnamon, which comes from Sri Lanka (it's ochre yellow and crumbly), if you can find it. Chinese cinnamon (the hard, dark brown sticks) is less sweet and more bitter. Cumin offers your baby a new flavour, and some believe it helps to soothe tummy aches.

Is it true that vanilla will help my baby sleep?

It has been suggested that vanilla does have sedative qualities. Just be sure not to give it to your children while they are younger than eight months old, and watch out for alcohol in vanilla extracts.

NUTRITIONAL INFORMATION

apple

An apple a day keeps the doctor away, right? Apples are known for containing compounds with anticancer and anticardiovascular disease properties. They are also a tasty souce of fibre.

apricot

This tiny fruit is one of the richest in provitamin A and trace elements. Two apricots alone supply half the daily requirement of carotene, a cancer-fighting antioxidant. Apricots also provide a large amount of potassium. Let's not forget the dried apricot's important contribution of iron, essential for little ones' development.

aubergine

With few calories and plenty of water, aubergines are equally rich in soft fibres called pectins, which gently aid digestion. If you find the laxative qualities in aubergines too strong, simply remove the seeds and skin. Don't forget that aubergines are rich in minerals (magnesium, zinc and manganese) with minimal levels of sodium – perfect for baby meals.

avocado

Extremely satiating and rich in healthy fats. Recent studies show the benefits of this fruit in treating liver problems. They're an equally excellent source of vitamins B5 (nerve impulses) and B6 (immune system).

banana

The banana is the champion of active babies; it's a very energising fruit (90 calories for 100g/3½ oz). It's important to note that the composition of this delectable fruit varies according to its maturity level. The riper the fruit, the less rich it is in vitamin C and starch and the more simple sugars it contains. Bananas are also chock-full of potassium, copper, magnesium and B vitamins.

basil

The ancient Greeks lauded the virtues of basil (*basilikon* means 'royal herb') for its numerous health qualities.

beef

Beef is a primary source for nutritional iron because it contains haem-iron, an iron that absorbs five times better than iron found in plants. Don't forget that growing children have a strong need for iron. Add to this that beef is an excellent source of ultra-high-quality protein and zinc. Remember, though, not to overdo it, because in large doses beef can be detrimental to the cardiovascular system, due to the presence of saturated fatty acids.

blueberry

This berry, very high in vitamin C (an antioxidant), has a protective and beneficial effect on vision. It is also said that blueberries have a beneficial effect on memory, and they are also rich in potassium and phosphorus.

broad beans

Low in calories, fresh broad beans have important nutritional qualities. They're high in fibre (a powerful laxative) and contain a good amount of potassium, magnesium and the B and C vitamins.

broccoli

This is a powerhouse of vitamin C: It contains twice the amount that an orange contains. In a 200g (7oz) portion, you get more than your recommended daily requirement. Broccoli is equally very rich in provitamins, known for their antioxidant properties. Plus, broccoli has very few calories.

carrot

Bugs Bunny, who ate carrots to keep an eye out for Elmer Fudd, knows it well· this orange root is rich in beta-carotene, for fortifying the retina and improving night vision. But the virtues of this royal vegetable don't stop there. Rich in carotene, substantial carrot consumption also provides nourishment for the skin.

cauliflower

Of all vegetables, cauliflower boasts one of the highest concentrations of minerals, notably magnesium and potassium. With few calories, it is also very rich in vitamin C: a 200g (7oz) portion covers the daily recommended amount.

celeriac

Very rich in minerals, this root vegetable contains trace elements rarely found in other vegetables: most notably selenium (immune booster) and chromium (which facilitates assimilation of sugars). It is also loaded with fibre and low in calories.

cherries

Juicy and very sweet, the cherry is a refreshing energy fruit. In addition, a big dose of vitamin C and provitamin A.

chestnut

Chestnuts, considered a starch, are nevertheless high in vitamins and minerals. A 200g (7oz) portion of cooked and mashed chestnuts meets 25 per cent of the daily recommended allowance of magnesium (a relaxant). But the real benefit lies in the fact that chestnuts don't contain gluten, an ideal food for babies and children who have a gluten intolerance.

cod

This white fish is exceptionally nutritious. It's low in lipids and carbohydrates and rich in selenium (anti-free radical) and phosphorus (bones and teeth). Don't forget that cod offers plenty of iodine, a trace element that regulates the thyroid gland, which is responsible for calorie combustion.

coriander

Sometimes called 'Chinese parsley', coriander has been used since antiquity for its digestive and carminative (antibloating/flatulence) virtues. Used as a herbal infusion, coriander is antidiarrhoeal and antispasmodic. Add to this its unique flavour and its important contribution of vitamin K (which aids in blood clotting and bone formation) and you understand why Eastern peoples honour it so.

courgettes

Though low in calories, courgettes are extremely high in minerals and vitamins such as A (beneficial to bones and teeth and an anti-infective), B (good for general growth and the immune system) and C (useful for healing and iron absorption). When eaten young, they contain particularly tender fibres, well suited for fragile digestive systems. The perfect vegetable for *les petits*!

cucumber

High in water content, cucumbers are swimming in minerals like potassium and phosphorus. They also provide B vitamins, necessary for healthy skin. Contrary to popular belief, cucumbers are easily digested and sit well in young tummies.

fennel

A good source of antioxidant vitamins (A and E), fennel is rich in soft fibre, which helps to activate the bowel and facilitates movement through the intestine. It also has anti-bloating properties that are ideal in cases of excess wind. And don't forget that unique aniseed-like flavour!

garlic

Not only does garlic enhance all kinds of dishes, its medicinal properties are unequalled: it combats hypertension and reduces cholesterol levels, reinforces immune defences and has anti-free radical properties. It's also a mine of trace elements like manganese, zinc and selenium. Add to this antibacterial, anti-allergenic and anti-tumour abilities.

grapes

No need to argue the well-known benefits of grapes. Very energising and nutritious, grapes nevertheless remain extremely digestible, perfect for a baby's immature digestive tract. High in vitamins A, B and C, they also contain magnesium and potassium.

green beans

Green beans contain vitamins and minerals. Rich in provitamin A (which is good for growth and the immune system), as well as C (which is good for healing) and E (which is anti-free radical). Green beans are also packed with potassium.

lamb

Lamb is a rather fatty meat – the lipid content varies according to the cut of the animal – but its rich flavour and good proteins largely compensate for this small inconvenience. Lamb is also rich in vitamin B12, which is anti-anaemic, and zinc, which is good for the heart and bones.

lemons

Sealed inside their thick skins, lemons are champions of vitamin C. Heavy on benefits, they are packed with potassium. They pair well with both savoury and sweet in the kitchen.

lentils

A super pulse, lentils are low in calories and have an incredible capacity to satiate without adding fat. They contain a record amount of minerals: much-needed iron being one of them. Rich in fibre, they are also good for combating constipation. Lentils contain a significant amount of vegetable protein (they rival meat protein when eaten with wholegrains) and you can understand why cooks serve them so often.

mangoes

The mango is teeming with vitamins – of all fruits, it contains the most antioxidants (a half a mango covers all daily requirements). It has high amounts of B vitamins (for growth), vitamin A, vitamin C (for iron absorption) and vitamin E (for the immune system). Also worth boasting about is this fruit's 80 per cent water content and its low calorie count.

melon

Though low in calories (they're 90 per cent water), melons are not light on benefits, thanks to their treasure trove of provitamin A (especially true of orange-coloured melons like cantaloupe) and vitamin C. High in fibre, they can be mildly laxative, especially when eaten cold.

mint

In addition to its antioxidant properties, mint has a lovely refreshing taste.

muesli

Muesli (from Swiss German *müesli*) is a blend of various cereals, grains and dried fruits according to taste. It's most often made of oats, wheat, rye and barley flakes and raisins, sometimes with walnuts, hazelnuts, linseeds, pecan nuts, or dried figs, depending on the season. The richness of the whole grains in muesli forms an incomparable source of fibre, proteins and energy. For babies, choose a type of muesli that does not have added sugar (you can always add honey or for children older than 12 months a lighter amount of sugar yourself).

nectarines

From the same family as the peach, nectarines boast many trace elements: phosphorus for the formation of bones, copper for tissue repair. Nectarines are rich in vitamins B3 (good for energy production), C (a powerful antioxidant) and E (useful for cell protection).

oats

This supergrain is rich in soluble fibres, whose effect on digestion and elimination is well known. Oats also have favourable effects on the regulation of cholesterol and blood-sugar levels. They're rich in proteins. In addition, oats are loaded with iron, phosphorus and magnesium and are rich in B vitamins.

oranges

Here's another vitamin C champion; one orange nearly covers the daily recommended allowance. Oranges contain a significant amount of soft fibres (ideal for difficult bowels), minerals and trace elements.

parsnips

This elongated fleshy root that looks like a big white carrot (the two have common origins) has impressive nutritional qualities. Along with its slight hazelnut flavour, the parsnip boasts complex sugars and fructose, which calm hunger quickly with a lasting effect. It's also high in potassium, vitamin C and folic acid (good for cell development and the nervous system).

pasta

Contrary to popular belief, pasta doesn't cause weight gain; its lipid content is extremely low. It's the accompaniments we eat with pasta that pile on the calories. Made from wheat, pasta contains starches that gradually release their energy. Perfect for mini-explorers on the go.

peaches

Loaded with the antioxidants vitamin C and beta-carotene, peaches are your skin's best friends. They have a high water content and very little sugar, making them ideal summer snacks. The soft fibres in peaches are particularly good for baby's fragile intestines and aid with constipation, especially when eaten raw.

pears

The fibre in pears helps with digestion. Pears have a high mineral content, including phosphorus and magnesium. They are also loaded with vitamin C and boast uncontested antioxidant virtues.

peas

Green peas are like beans: packed with energy and perfect for mini-athletes. Their protein and vitamin B content is almost five times greater than other fresh vegetables. Peas also happen to be full of minerals such as potassium and phosphorus, as well as trace elements (copper, zinc and fluoride).

peppers

Cousins to chilli peppers (but without the spice), peppers are the fresh vegetable with the most vitamin C. It was actually in the sweet pepper that A. Szent-Györgyi, a Hungarian scientist, first discovered vitamin C in the 1930s. Peppers are an excellent source of carotene and vitamin E, antioxidants known for preventing cancer and cardiovascular disease.

pineapple

Rich in minerals, pineapples have a high vitamin C content despite their moderate calorie count. But the pineapple's major benefit is the presence of bromelain, an enzyme that is reputed to activate and facilitate the digestion of proteins.

plums

Their sweetness depends on the variety and the plum's maturity, but all plums are high in B vitamins and provitamin A, which is involved in cell growth and protection. The fruit pigments considerably reinforce the power of vitamin C. Plums are also high in potassium, magnesium and several other trace elements. Rich in soluble and insoluble fibre, plums aid with digestion and gently combat slow bowels.

yellow (mirabelle) plums

If you are lucky enough to find them, Mirabelle plums are little and yellow, juicy, sweet and deliciously perfumed. They are very rich in trace elements and vitamins B and E.

pumpkin

Almost 90 per cent water, pumpkins have few calories. Their ample potassium content helps prevent kidney stones as well as hypertension. Low in sodium, they're good for feeding Bébé, who can't withstand a heavy salt intake. Like carrots, pumpkins are well endowed with provitamin A – one portion of pumpkin covers the daily recommended allowance for an adult.

raspberries

Low in calories and slightly acidic, raspberries are the perfect summer dessert. High in fibre, they can have laxative effects. Sensitive tummies prefer them puréed into a fruit coulis and strained of their seeds. Raspberries offer many minerals, including potassium and magnesium. They're also rich in vitamin C and flavonoids (which are helpful to blood circulation).

rice

After wheat, rice is the most consumed grain in the world. Very satisfying, it's also prized for its nutritional value. It's rich in magnesium and contains phosphorus, zinc, B vitamins and potassium. Rice has antidiarrhoeal effects – especially its cooking water

saffron

Saffron has long been reputed to remedy ailments. The pigment responsible for its deep red-orange colour also stimulates digestion. Saffron is also thought to have analgesic and sedative qualities, perfect for troubled sleep or anxiety. North African folk remedies for teething pains are made from honey and saffron.

sage

Known as the 'marvellous plant' by the ancient Gauls of France, sage possesses incomparable anti-inflammatory powers, wound-healing abilities and tonic, digestive and antiseptic properties too.

salmon

Whether wild or farmed, salmon has exceptional nutritional virtues. It's a fatty ('good fat') fish that's extremely rich in omega-3, one of the essentials for your baby's brain development. Salmon contributes an ample amount of iron, phosphorus and magnesium as well as a significant amount of vitamins A (for vision, growth and immune defences) and D (for teeth and bones).

strawberries

Besides its one-of-a-kind flavour, which happens to be the favourite of children everywhere, the strawberry is packed with folic acid (beneficial for the immune system), beta-carotene (helpful for cell renewal) and vitamin C (useful as an antioxidant). It's also rich in trace elements like potassium (valuable for the nervous system) and magnesium (helpful as a relaxant), as they can cause allergic reactions.

swede

The swede is a cross between the cabbage and the turnip. It's rich in potassium, phosphorus and vitamin C. In addition, swede is low in calories. It's also been ascribed digestive virtues and is a reputed intestinal disinfectant.

sweet potato

Originally from South America before growers cultivated them in the Caribbean, sweet potatoes resemble regular potatoes in many culinary ways (however, with the addition of an undoubtable sweetness). And they clearly stand apart when compared nutritionally. Sweet potatoes possess a very low rating on the glycaemic index and offer a contribution in provitamin A – a powerful antioxidant.

sweetcorn

Rarely used in baby food (unfortunately), sweetcorn is a valuable food low in lipids but high in fibre, the B vitamins (for growth) and phosphorus (for bones and teeth). It also packs a powerful antioxidant punch.

tarragon

A herb known for its full-bodied, hint-of-liquorice flavour, tarragon is thought to be an appetite stimulant with digestive and anti-bloating properties.

thyme

Thyme is a real multipurpose medicine. It is reputed to stimulate the appetite and guard against bloating while offering antibacterial and even antiseptic properties. Try it as a herbal infusion to treat minor colds.

tomato

With a very high water content (95 per cent), tomatoes are low in calories and an excellent source of minerals. They're full of potassium (good for combating hypertension), magnesium, zinc and phosphorus. Tomatoes are also an excellent source of vitamins A, B and C. Perhaps their best asset is their gorgeous red colour, which comes from the lycopene they contain. In humans this precious pigment protects cells from free radical attack and plays an important role as an antioxidant and preventer of some kinds of cancer.

vanilla

Besides its wonderfully sweet flavour, vanilla is thought to possess sedative qualities and is sometimes used as a herbal infusion or with aromatherapy to calm troubled sleep. A recent study conducted at the Hospital of Strasbourg and led by Luc Marlier (of the French National Centre for Scientific Research) demonstrated that premature babies exposed to the scent of vanilla had more regular breathing patterns and were 45 per cent less likely to experience sleep apnoea. The scent of vanilla enticed babies to suckle, nurse and relax. Use it to prepare for a good night's sleep!

NOTES

Acknowledgements

I am truly proud of this personal recipe book, which was – until now – just a workbook, written by hand, worn out and full of stains. Today that workbook has become this book thanks to the many people who put up with me: testers, supporters, sources of inspiration, editors and so on.

Huge thanks first of all to Marabout, to Emmanuel and Amaryllis, who gave me the opportunity to write this book and who believed in me. Thanks to them, this book is really beautiful, personal and original. Thanks also to Fred and Sonia Lucano for the magnificent photographs and to the baby models who really got into the spirit. And a giant *merci* to Cédrine Meier – who, thanks to her formidable talent for writing, helped me make the text readable, relevant and funny.

Great thanks, as well, to my friend Dr Jean Lalau Keraly, who has supported me from the very first day, who is always to hand with advice and who is extremely generous with his time.

I also want to pay homage to my husband, David, who through his support, tolerance and involvement in our family allowed me to throw myself into the crazy adventure that is Baby Meals (Les Menus Bébé), as well as work day and night on this book.

Finally, the biggest thanks of all to my children, Maya and Milo. You are my reason for living and my inspiration. All of this is thanks to you. I love you like crazy!

Thanks to White and Brown household appliances.

All the babies in this book were dressed by Lily & the Funky Boys. Thanks, Esther!

	around 6 months	6 months+	9 months+	12 months+
APPLES	26, 34	55, 66		126, 160, 165
APRICOTS	28	52	86	107
AUBERGINE		64	86, 87	
AVOCADO	41			124
BANANAS	32			146, 151, 156, 160
BEEF		59		108, 109
BLUEBERRIES		70		
BROAD BEANS		62	93	118, 125
BROCCOLI	38	53, 58		
BUTTERNUT SQUASH			83	
CARROTS	36	52, 56, 59, 63, 67	82, 86	104, 106, 107, 109, 122, 124, 136
CAULIFLOWER	44			
CELERIAC		57, 58		126
CHERRIES	34	70		
CHERRY TOMATOES				116, 125, 128, 133, 134
CLEMENTINES		74		151
COCONUT MILK				104, 136, 142
COURGETTES		53, 58, 59, 62, 64	86, 87, 90, 93	104, 106, 107, 109, 122
FENNEL		56, 57, 63		
FIGS				161
FISH		60, 61, 62, 63, 64		110, 116, 118, 120
GINGER		55	86	104, 106, 136, 142
GREEN BEANS	40	53, 58	90	104, 120, 138
GREEN GRAPES		63		151
GREEN LENTILS			94	
HAM				112, 114
HONEY				140, 146, 148, 149, 156, 161
LAMB		58		107
LYCHEE	33			160
MANGO	32	73, 74		146, 151, 156, 160
MELON	29	74		150
MILK CHOCOLATE				164
MINT		72		149
MUESLI				146, 148, 149
NECTARINES		73		
ONIONS		54		108

	around 6 months	6 months+	9 months+	12 months+
ORANGES		74		116
ORANGE JUICE	36	52, 56, 63	84	106, 122
PARMESAN		69	80	113, 125, 128, 132, 135
PARSNIPS	43	57, 63		126
PASTA			88	112, 130, 132, 133, 134, 135
PEACHES	24	74		150, 156
PEARS	27, 35			161
PEAS	39	58	90	112, 114, 120, 130, 135, 138, 140
PEPPER (SPICE)				108, 109
PEPPERS (VEGETABLE)				128, 134, 138, 142
PINEAPPLE	33			
PLUMS	35			
POTATOES	45, 46	60, 66, 68		108, 120
POULTRY		52, 53, 54, 55		104, 106, 113, 114
PUMPKIN	45	66	96	142
PRUNES				164
RAISINS/SULTANAS		63		106, 146, 154, 164
RASPBERRIES		72		149, 150, 156, 162, 166
RED LENTILS				122, 136
RICE			80	113, 138, 142
SEMOLINA		69	84	110
SOFT CHEESE			88, 98	
SPINACH		61	92, 94	
STRAWBERRIES		72		150, 156, 162, 165
SUGAR SNAP PEAS				135
SWEDE		57		126
SWEET POTATOES	42	60	96	114, 142
SWEETCORN	46	54	99	124, 138
TOMATOES		59, 64	82, 86, 87, 91, 99	106, 107, 108, 109, 126, 128, 136
TURNIPS		53, 58, 68		
VANILLA POD				96, 152, 153, 161, 162
VEAL		56, 57		
WATERMELON		74		
WHOLEGRAIN BREAD				158, 160, 161
YELLOW PLUM	30			148
YOGURT		70		122, 152, 156